LOVE

The Ultimate Answer to the Meaning of Life

edited by Nicolae Tanase

Published and distributed in the United States, Canada, United Kingdom, Germany, France, Italy, Spain, Netherlands, India, Japan, Brazil, Mexico, Australia by Kindle Direct Publishing.
Imprint: Independently published.

ISBN: 9781983205095 (paperback, ebook)

Contents

Preface

What is the meaning of life?

They say it's Love!

The love molecule, the feast of love, the grand reunion, the song of the soul, the universal force of love, the experience of true love, heartbeats, breath, destiny, chocolates, pure unlimited love, the breath of life, the art of love and faith, eternal light, the gift of unconditional love, remembering the divine source, beloved, Rumi, whispers of the heart, soaring as a soul, the wisdom of the heart, pouring love... that's what awaits you between the pages of this book. For Love alone is the Greatest Power.

Between 2015 and 2018 I asked more than a thousand renowned and spiritual people from around the world one question: *what is the meaning of life?*

This book is an anthology of about 60 timeless answers on *Love* as the *Meaning of Life.*

This book is a journey... a journey into the sap of life, into the deep roots of love. It is a book that can be read over and over and over and over..... with no ends... for love is within and it is without, it is like the fragrance of a flower.

It is a book which describes that which needs to be lived and felt. It is a book that needs to be breathed.

Enjoy the quintessence of life... and immerse yourself into the infinite ocean of love.

Acknowledgements

I'm only the editor of this book and express deep gratitude to every author who took the time to contribute their thoughts and/or beliefs on *Love* and the *Meaning of Life*.

I would also like to thank the authors' assistants, agents, publishers, colleagues and friends who provided support and cooperated with me during the *Meaning of Life* journey.

Nicolae Tanase – the editor
June, 2018

To the life on Earth...

The Ultimate Reply to the Meaning of Life?
by Pierre Pradervand

When asked the question *what is the meaning of life?*, I would be tempted to reply, "I don't know". Every day, I am more and more in awe about this incredible place called "the universe" we live in. And every day, I am more and more aware of my quasi abysmal ignorance of what "reality" really (!) is. So my only honest reply is to explain what the meaning of life is for me. That is just one reply among the 7,7 billion inhabitants of our little planet which does not give it an immense weight but it does cause me to wake up each day with a song of gratitude in my heart for another day of loving.

The deeper meaning of life for me is far beyond the comprehension of that fabulous but incredibly limited tool called the human mind. It has to be felt on the level of the heart. For me, it was birthed in the most powerful mystical experience of my life.

Many years ago I was attending the board meeting of the largest grass roots peasant-farmer movement in Africa, of which I was a founding member, in Ouhigouya (Burkina-Faso in the Sahel).

The last day of the meeting I contracted dysentery and as at the time I was following a path of pure spiritual healing I worked on it spiritually. On the plane the next day I was still working on the issue with my spiritual texts, affirmations, prayers and the like. Next to me was an unaccompanied young boy, and the stewardess caring for him was the incarnation of love. At one moment she spoke to him with such kindness I was suddenly overwhelmed by what I can only describe as a sort of cosmic gratitude which enveloped her and everything.

And suddenly, I was projected into a space which was timeless and beyond material space, and where I was aware of nothing else but infinite Love. I felt in my very essence that unconditional Love was the only cause, effect, substance, power, being, reality, identity, presence in the universe, that it was literally All-in-all.

The most wonderful thing of the whole experience is that my ego had completely disappeared. I had no sense anymore that anyone called Pierre Pradervand even existed. For an indeterminate period (as I was no longer in time) the divine consciousness WAS my consciousness, which is why this was the most glorious experience of my existence: infinite love manifesting as total freedom. *The human mind (intellect, mental reign) had just vanished*, all was on the level of this extraordinary feeling of the divine.

And suddenly, I was back in my seat on the plane. I felt something moving in my bowels and in a matter of seconds, the dysentery had disappeared.

But that healing, however welcome, was nothing compared to the vision which brought with it a quality of knowing that human words just cannot describe – because it was far beyond normal human experience. I now feel with such a depth of certainty, of spiritual groundedness that Love is the ultimate reply to all and any problem, be it personal, social or a world issue.

And you and I are one with that Love. We are literally welded to Love and nothing will ever be able to change that, even our own doubts and fears. Love is our home, our haven, our springboard and our resting place – for always.

Because we are literally divine Love expressing itself.

NOW.

❧❧❧

Pierre Pradervand

During a professional life span of over fifty years spent in many cultures and countries on the five continents, Pierre has practiced occupations as varied as sociologist, international consultant, journalist, trainer and writer amongst others. He now lives in his native Switzerland where he runs workshops on personal development and spirituality at 7000 feet in an old chalet in the Swiss alps. He does a great deal of volunteering and his aim for many years has been a win-win world that works for all.

www.gentleartofblessing.org

www.pierrepradervand.com

LOVE and the Meaning of Life
by Kahlil Gibran

Life without Love is like a tree without blossom and fruit. And love without Beauty is like flowers without scent and fruits without seeds... Life, Love, and Beauty are three persons in one, who cannot be separated or changed.

The spiritual awakening is the most essential thing in man's life, and it is the sole purpose of being.

The Reality of Life is Life itself, whose beginning is not in the womb, and whose ending is not in the grave. For the years that pass are naught but a moment in eternal life; and the world of matter and all in it is but a dream compared to the awakening which we call the terror of Death.

Vain are the beliefs and teachings that make man miserable, and false is the goodness that leads him into sorrow and despair, for it is man's purpose to be happy on this earth and lead the way to felicity and preach its gospel wherever he goes. He who does not see the kingdom of heaven in this life will never see it in the coming life. We came not into this life by exile, but we came as innocent creatures of God, to learn how to worship the holy and eternal spirit and seek the hidden secrets within ourselves from the beauty of life.

The true light is that which emanates from within man, and reveals the secrets of the heart to the soul, making it happy and contented with life.

Love is my sole entertainer, singing songs of happiness for me at night and waking me at dawn to reveal the meaning of life and the secrets of nature. An eternal hunger for love and beauty is my desire. I know now that those who possess bounty alone are naught but miserable, but to my spirit the sighs of lovers are more soothing than music of the lyre.

I came to live in the glory of Love and the light of Beauty, which are the reflections of God. I am here living, and the people are unable to exile me from the domain of life for they know I will live in death. If they pluck my eyes I will hearken to the murmurs of Love and the songs of Beauty.

Love is the only freedom in the world because it so elevates the spirit that the laws of humanity and the phenomena of nature do not alter its course. Love is a divine knowledge that enables men to see as much as the gods.

Love is a power that makes our hearts, yet our hearts cannot make that power.

Love gives naught but itself and takes naught but from itself. Love possesses not nor would it be possessed. For love is sufficient unto love.

Limited love asks for possession of the beloved, but the unlimited asks only for itself. Love that comes between the naiveté and awakening of youth satisfies itself with possessing, and grows with embraces. But Love which is born in the firmament's lap and has descended with the night's secrets is not contended with anything but Eternity and immortality; it does not stand reverently before anything except deity.

"I was deeply engrossed in thought and contemplation and seeking to understand the meaning of nature and the revelation of books and scriptures when I heard LOVE whispered into my ears through Selma's lips. My life was a coma, empty like that of Adam's in Paradise, when I saw Selma standing before me like a column of light. She was the Eve of my heart who filled it with secrets and wonders and made me understand the meaning of life."

~*The Broken Wings*

Khalil Gibran was a Lebanese-American writer, poet and visual artist.Gibran is the third best-selling poet of all time, behind Shakespeare and Laozi.

The Love Molecule
by Paul J. Zak

Love is the meaning of life. Full stop.

Love is the highest aspiration, the most valued emotion, and the one that hurts us to the core when it is taken away.

"But," you must be thinking, "this isn't new." Nearly every love song on the radio tells us we should be living for love. Many religious and philosophical traditions say the same.

What is new is the science.

My lab was the first to show that the neurochemical of love, oxytocin, is synthesized in the brain when we are shown a kindness by a stranger. In a dozen years of research, we have shown that nearly any positive social interaction causes the brain to make oxytocin and oxytocin, in turn, motivates us to treat others with care and compassion. In short, the "love molecule" oxytocin is quietly signaling who we should care about.

All four types of love identified by the Greek philosophers seem to stimulate the brain to make oxytocin. These are: romantic love (eros), parent-child love (storge), friendship (philia), and love for God or some transcendent ideal (agape). Demonstrating tangible care for others is how we express of love. This is precisely what oxytocin causes us to do: to reach out and connect to those around us.

My research has two really exciting take-aways. First, because oxytocin is active in evolutionary old parts of the brain, human beings appear to be designed to constantly find opportunities to love others. Love is a deep part of our human nature. By embracing this nature we are true to ourselves and are more fulfilled in our lives.

Second, the more one's brain makes oxytocin, the more we are predisposed to make it. In other words, the more we love others, the more easily we love. And when we love others, their brains produce oxytocin and they show love in return. You have got to give love to get it, and our brains make this easier to do as we mature.

My years of research and especially my efforts to apply my findings to create a more compassionate world have earned me the nickname Dr. Love. If you'll allow Dr. Love to offer you some advice, here it is: tell one person today that you love them. This could be a friend, parent, child, work colleague, teacher, or neighbor. If "love" is too scary, then substitute "appreciate." Do this for one new person a week and you'll be stimulating their brains to make oxytocin and creating a more loving world. That could just add meaning to your life.

Paul J. Zak, PhD is a scientist, prolific author, and public speaker. He is the founding Director of the *Center for Neuroeconomics Studies and Professor of Economics, Psychology and Management at Claremont Graduate University.* Dr. Zak also serves as Professor of Neurology at Loma Linda University Medical Center. He is credited with the first published use of the term "neuroeconomics" and has been a vanguard in this new discipline.
www.PaulJZak.com

The Feast of Love
by Dan Furst

Everybody's heard, because every tradition has them, the stories of the one who's hungry for truth, usually a boy, who goes to ask the famous sage, usually a solitary old man, to tell him the meaning of life. The answer is never just around the corner.

It's always an ordeal. The seeker crosses a desert, like the Prophet Muhammad, Peace Be Upon Him. Or he braves a dark forest, like Dante, or, like the Buddha, he lives for years with stricter-than-thou ascetics who scorn him for eating a few grains of rice. Or the journey may take years of emotional hardship, as it did in the mystery school of Pythagoras, where students had to spend three years as *exoterikoi* (those "outside the veil") and endure a year of silence before they got inside the veil, as *esoterikoi*, and got to see the Master face to face for the first time. We can imagine how carefully framed the student's first question must have been.

Or the truth hunter has to go uphill, like Moses, Jesus, and Milarepa. The mountain always has a grand mythic charge because the climb is harder, going up against gravity, and it takes us up above the coarseness and heaviness of the Earth, closer to the air realm of birds and angels, and ultimately toward the pure bliss and freedom of the Divine.

When the seeker at last finds the holy one, seated on sheepskins at the front of his cave, and asks him for the meaning of life, the old man pauses, nods, and then asks, "Did you set out on your own to come here? Or did you tell your family and friends? Did they think you're crazy? Did you think the same thing maybe halfway up the trail, and wonder how you could imagine doing this? Was it much harder than you expected? Did you see any animals on your way up? Did any of them approach you, call to you, even touch you? Did you hear what the wind said? Was there a message in the rain? Did any plants address you, even by name?"

The young man does his best to answer all of these. He especially wonders why the old man wants to know more about the dead fox with the wound exposing its entrails, and about the smell of wild thyme at the narrowest pat of the trail. The seeker keeps trying to pull the thread back to the meaning of life, without getting impatient, but to no avail. The old man apparently wants to get to everything but the point, and his new student now has a lot more questions than the one he came with.

He asks himself: is this man really a failed comedian who has usurped the old wise one's cave, and hidden him somewhere? If so, where? If not, yow! If I stay on this path, am I going to be like this in another 60 years, and will I be so indirect that I'm practically dishonest? Why does he want to know everything I thought and felt on my way up here, especially the things I don't like about myself, and most of all my memories of the things I did that really hurt other people?

By the time the old man says you can stay the night in my cave, there's no way you get back down the mountain before dark, the young man is starting to get it. He sees that anyone who tries to answer a question that big, and serve it to him on a plate, even on a flat rock or a strip of bark, is not helping him, but robbing him of the insight that can come only from within after a right effort to find it. The young man thanks the sage for doing exactly what he was supposed to do by stoking a hunger that can't be satisfied in the mind with thoughts and words, or even in the heart for long, not even with the pure food of love, joy and bliss — unless the feast of truth is shared with others.

The young pilgrim sees for himself, farther down the road when the time is right, the answer that lights up each of us, and brings the love out of us: that The Meaning of Life will look different to each of us, but our images of it will have common features:

The broad forehead of a world view that sees awareness and compassion going wide, beyond families and friends, even communities and countries, to global and even galactic resonances in a holistic design that embraces all.

The eyes that mirror the luminosity, beauty and joy of each one we meet.

The ears that listen more than the mouth speaks.

The smile of acceptance in the comedy of life, that knows all are included, every role is important, all crisis and drama are fleeting, and in the end all are welcomed in the feast of love.

❧❧❧

Dan Furst is an actor, ceremonial artist, author and astrologer specializing in astrocartography, the subject of his new books *Finding Your Best Places* (2015) and *Maps of Power* (due in 2016). He is an Aquarian activist who aims to contribute what he can to the communal awakening of consciousness. www.DanFurst.com

An Endless Embrace
by Kari Hohne

I find meaning with nature as my teacher. The sun offers a curriculum of how to rise each day, activating a chain reaction of abundance by simply shining. When we light the fire of love in our heart, we smile, and the world responds with love. The moon reminds us of our power to reflect light for others in their times of darkness. Trees are the masters of not playing the host, but remain the guest of what life brings to us. Grass demonstrates how we are all connected at our roots and thrive by supporting each other. Birds remind us that the song in our heart is more real than any song we hear around us. Like the earth, we succumb to autumn, stripped of the known where we turn inward to winter in our underworld, reconnecting with our roots.

I believe when we dream we enter the world of the Shaman and achieve second sight. So much goes on below the surface that orchestrates manifestation and there is much about the hidden side of life we will never know. Like another organ of digestion, when we dream we assimilate what we need and discard the self inhibiting ideas that stunt our forward progress. Animals dream and they too are learning something and have a right to be here. After winter, we rise again in field of seeds that become the 10,000 flowers of spring. How beautiful we are!

A gardener will tell you that growth is not always measured by what we receive, but how well we allow the unnecessary to be pruned away. What will it be next year? It may be similar, but it won't be the same. So meaning is a dandelion seed blowing in the wind to become tomorrow's dream. But there is some aspect of us visible in our childhood that always remains the same, and we need to make it our alter.

I don't believe there is anything negative happening in nature, even with floods, hurricanes and forest fires. Nature is committed to life and has been fostering our success since the day we were born, even when we have yet to understand the why of the pathway. When we are lost – we are just here and that is such a wonderful place to be. Our universe seems to have a predisposition for the unknown and opening to wonder keeps us free. Nature continuously pulls us into its flow of abundance.

So the meaning of life to me, is not to take anything so seriously that we miss out on living and forget we are natural creatures being shaped by natural processes. And I don't believe we are an organic being at odds with our spiritual self. I think when we embrace our nature self, our human-ness and remove all boundaries that separate us from all we see – we are just this and it is beautiful. Only we know what it means to be fearlessly ourselves. And it is always perfect. I celebrate you!

Namaste...let us dance with the Shadow until we both fall down laughing in an endless embrace.

❧❀❀❧❀

Kari Hohne is the lead artist in Get Tribal, and the creator of www.CafeauSoul.com

The Light of Divine Love
by Martha St. Claire

We are here to make a difference, to touch hearts, to heal others and ourselves, and to accelerate consciousness. We are here to love one another back to the Divine and along the way, to co-create Heaven on Earth.

During my last near-death experience, in a space of extreme clarity and Heavenly bliss, it all made so much sense.

We come from the Divine, we return to that endless Light, and in between, we are always one with God, Source, and All That Is, capable of sharing great light and love, just by the sacred nature of our beings, and capable of being agents of wonderful change in a world seemingly desperate for compassion, love, and understanding.

Our eternal souls choose this existence for a time and there truly is a divine plan and higher order to things, contrary to appearances.

In the midst of hugely challenging times on our planet, we may be filled with great doubt and confusion. We may feel anything but holy, trusting, and connected.

We may wonder who and what we are, life can seem unfair, and some may even question the existence of God, a higher consciousness, an after-life, or simply   basic goodness in others. We may have a hard time being kind to ourselves or self-accepting.

Often, my human self feels caught in an endless to-do-list, worn down by everyday tasks and limited by the illusion of a lack of time and I think, "Is this the only meaning to my life?!"

Yet, in transcended moments, I feel bliss and a sense of living out of normal time and space, and that all is well in the midst of an ordinary appearing day, in spite of how the world is and my related big concern and sadness.

In tough moments, we can breathe, be still, and choose to sense and seek the divine love that is always there for us and send that tangible peace and transforming love to others, if we but will.

The meaning of life is contained within a sacred fire, ever in the depths of our beings seeking to infuse our souls with that which was there all along. We have within an electric light of pure divine love, the greatest force in the universe, always at our beckon call.

You are an angel of infinite hope and goodness. You are part of a higher plan and vast universe that ever seeks to remind you and adore you. Life cherishes you, is grateful for you, and you give great meaning to life, just by being you! You are life!

May your light shine ever brightly, knowing that you are never alone, blessed by more than perhaps meets the eye.

❧᪥᪥

Martha St. Claire M.A., is a Near-Death Experience educator, hospital health care professional, and intuitive counselor. As a near-death experiencer and Gerontologist, Martha is especially interested in end of life issues and the after-life. She has served on the International Association for Near-Death Studies (IANDS) Board of Directors (2001-2003).

In addition, Martha is an evidential spiritual medium bringing comfort and connection for clients who long to be in touch with loved ones and pets who have passed on. She brings a greater awareness of Heaven and transformational guidance for one's daily life and soul path. Martha has been featured in the media, on television and in film documentaries, the news, radio, the internet, and print media
www.MarthaStClaire.com

The Art of Love and Faith
by Michael Finkelstein

I've been consciously working on this question since I turned 10. I remember that exact day vividly, and though I wasn't very old at the time, I began to wonder about our experience of mortality and why we had to die. Indeed, I felt an insistent ticking of the clock from that moment on – pressure to figure it out, or at least, to figure out how to live meaningfully.

Over the years, I've come to realize that the "meaning of life question" can be looked at from two perspectives: the individual and the collective. By examining each and by integrating the two, I feel we get closer to the essence of why the question is so significant. And, this is important, because by themselves, though each question has value, we are lead into an incomplete and limited understanding, as in most either-or scenarios. Instead, since both perspectives exist simultaneously, the ultimate answer to such a universal question must be inclusive of both.

To help understand how this works, I often point to the life of bees. When you look at the colony you can certainly identify the individuals, giving them individual names, such as: Queen, Worker, Drone, and Brood. Yet, we also know that though they exist on this level, each with a role to play, if you will, a life with meaning; in fact, their greater service is to the collective. And that collective, as it turns out, works in service to an even greater one, in this case the ecosystem of the entire planet.

And so are we, as individuals and a collective, the latter in service to something greater. So, we can look at the question from these two perspectives, the individual and the collective. For me, the meaning of life then is about weaving the life of the individual into the life of the collective, in service to the whole. But, there is more to it — we are more significant than the bees.

With our soaring consciousness, we have expansive awareness — awareness of the bees and billions of other life forms and processes that constitute the cosmos. And, awareness of our own mortality, a condition that drives us to this question about meaning. Our role goes well beyond that of any other species on this planet. Indeed, it appears that we are the conscious connection between the Earth and all that lies beyond. Far more than just its physical aspects.

Further, not only does the question burns in our minds, it burns in our bodies, in the form of pain and suffering. Indeed, people often struggle with this reality, going so far as to question the creator about some perverted motive behind it. I understand how that might appear. Clearly, the ultimate answer to the question must also adjudicate the harsh reality of our limited and painful physical lives. After years of study and practice in medicine, as frustrating as it is not to be able to relieve all the suffering I have witnessed, I have come to appreciate how creative those who suffer become. And, it is in this that I surmise the point. We are a manifestation of creation that creates more as a result of the ephemeral nature of the physical body that houses our consciousness.

What do we create? Not so much the technology, nor the temporary remedies that that provides; but something more enduring....our art and expressions of love and faith.

And, this is my understanding, as much as I'd like to eliminate pain and our questioning as to why it exists at all, it seems that it has an essential purpose to the cosmic collective and ultimately the very explanation for our existence itself.

Only through our physical senses, and its inherent fragility, the pain receptors in the flesh and the incessant drumbeat of time running out banging around inside our heads, do we have the urgency to find relief, and in so doing, get creative the way we do. In the end, then, it is not about how much work we do, how good we are or what we learn; but instead, to simply live expressing our love. On a cosmic level that must contribute to the greater (cosmic) evolution that we are an integral part of.

And, so, our part, in the big play, is to express our love, through thick and thin, 'til death do us part.

As I wrote after a meditation about five years ago:

If I were God, I would make a man and a woman;
I would send my love for them into the stars
And pray they became dust.
The dust that will generate new planets
Seeding the soul of new life —
Going beyond my imagination toward my spirit;
The spirit that sings of a future that lies in your heart.

❧❧

Michael Finkelstein, MD, FACP, ABIHM, aka **The Slow Medicine Doctor®**, is the founder and executive director of The Slow Medicine Foundation and is the founder and medical director of SunRaven: The Home of Slow Medicine, a wellness center located on a farm, in Bedford, NY. Dr. Finkelstein is a medical blogger for Doctor Oz, Sharecare, and The Huffington Post; he is the author of *Slow Medicine: Hope and Healing for Chronic Illness*, endorsed by Andrew Weil, MD and Mehmet Oz, MD.
www.SlowMedicineDoctor.com

The Mystery, the Miracle, the Wonder of it All
by Ruben Habito

Nicolae Tanase: Professor Habito, what is the meaning of life

Ruben Habito: Allow me to respond not as a "professor" but as one human being just like yourself, just like everyone else for whom this question is unavoidable, and looms large in our minds. It confronts us every day as we course through our life journey here on earth, though we may not always be thinking about it. After all these years of having had this question in my heart since my youth, and pondering and struggling with it through the ups and downs of my own life, this is what comes up for me:

There is no "meaning of life" apart from living it, breath by breath, moment by moment, one day at a time, grateful for the mystery, the miracle, the wonder of it all.

It is waking up and welcoming the new day, washing one's face, getting dressed, smelling the coffee, taking breakfast. It is going off to work, saying "Good morning!" to colleagues, buckling down to business, taking a lunch break, back again to the office for more work, taking a break, checking out at five. It is getting back home, relaxing a bit, taking a walk outside, preparing dinner, smelling the aroma of what's cooking from the kitchen, enjoying the food with family, fixing up, doing the dishes, listening to music, reading a bit, getting tired, going to bed.

It is seeing a child smile, and smiling back. It is looking up at the blue sky, and seeing the clouds, feeling glad that the sun is shining. It is looking at the trees, the houses in the neighborhood, people walking their dogs, children playing in the park. On another day, it is hearing the ominous thunder, seeing the flash of lightning from the corner of my eye, rushing for shelter as the rain starts to fall, wiping my shoes on the rug in front of the door, watching the raindrops from my window, being glad I'm dry and safe inside.

It is playing with the kids, watching over them when they're sick, being relieved when the fever subsides. It is seeing a son or daughter off to college with a mixed feeling of relief and nostalgia, recalling those times when he or she was just a toddler. It is taking care of an elderly parent, speaking a little more loudly or repeating what you just said for the umpteenth time so they may understand. It is spending time with friends, eating out together, trading corny jokes and laughing out loud. It is watching a film with a loved one, holding hands during the movie. It is visiting a sick friend, feeling concerned, making small talk not knowing what else to say. It is losing a job, feeling despondent, finding a new one, changing career. It is counting the pennies, trying to make ends meet. It is saving up for a vacation, going on a splurge every now and then.

It is watching the news and getting troubled by what's happening in our world. It is lamenting for those who just died on a boat off the coast of Greece as they sought to flee their country seeking a better life elsewhere. It is feeling angry and helpless as another school shooting is announced in the news. It is feeling a numbing ache deep in my gut in reading about the melting polar ice caps, about the thousands of species are dying and disappearing from this Earth every year, about the rainforests being depleted. It is signing a petition to support a cause, writing a letter to a senator to urge some action on a matter one feels strongly about. It is joining a peace march, joining a rally for a cause of justice.

It is being hurt by a thoughtless comment of an acquaintance, and keeping it to oneself, not snapping back, though tempted to. It is feeling glad and grateful at hearing a kind word, at being appreciated for little favors done for another. It is buying a card to send to a friend for a birthday, or texting to convey greetings. It is attending a memorial service, saddened at the loss.

In the midst of all these ordinary things that happen from day to day, it is being stunned every now and then, by the mystery, the wonder, the beauty of it all. Without knowing why or where from, it is having the firmly rooted sense of being accepted, being cared for, of being loved. Empowered by this, it is living one's life just wanting to love back. It is being gifted with a glimpse of a boundless and timeless horizon opening up right here in this moment, in every here and now. It is the simple and quiet joy of just being, just as one is, grateful to be alive, and earnestly wishing from the heart, "may all be well, may all beings be well!"

It is growing old, getting sick, feeling weak, forgetting things. And when the time comes to bow out, heaving a last breath, with palms joined, heart filled with boundless gratitude, for this wondrous ride that is called life. Throughout all this, it is knowing deep, deep within, that somehow, in the final scheme of things, all shall be well, all manner of thing shall be well.

❧❀❧

Ruben L.F. Habito is a former Jesuit priest turned master practicing in the Sanbo Kyodan lineage of Zen. He is professor of World Religions and Spirituality at Perkins School of Theology, and founder of Maria Kannon Zen Center, Dallas, Texas.
www.mkzc.org

The Well Being of All Life on Earth
by Tina Malia

Years ago, someone told me a story that was passed down to him, that I'd like to share with you as well. The story goes that when the people of this particular Native American tribe entered the tipi and sat around the fire to pray, they did not pray for their own health, wealth, personal gain and woes. Instead, they prayed for those around them — their friends, neighbors, children, elders and relatives — that they would be bestowed with peace, happiness, joy; that they'd have bountiful harvests, clean water to drink, healthy bodies and minds.

They prayed for those around them to be filled with abundant love, shelter, and a sense of purpose and pride. In this way, everyone in the tipi was taken care of, everyone was prayed for, everyone's well being was the personal concern of those around them. There was no need to pray for yourself, as by caring for others it was ensured that your own life was also being watched over with great fervor by those around you.

I think of this story often, and as I ponder the meaning of life, I can't help but go back to this simple wisdom. It is so basic, yet holds so many keys to filling the void that so often accompanies modern day living.

So.....let's reach out. Let's show that we care about the people in our lives, beautify our home for unexpected guests, make life a little easier for someone that could use a helping hand, and mostly, let's pray for each other and the well being of all life on Earth. There will be so much purpose, so much meaning, it will be pouring out of every cell like a great tidal wave of love.

❧✿❀✿❀

Tina Malia is a visionary musical artist. Her sonic creations span folk, world, dream pop and sacred music genres. A prolific singer, songwriter, instrumentalist and sound engineer, Malia expresses her radiant inner landscape through song.
www.TinaMalia.com

The Universal Force is LOVE
Albert Einstein

In the late 1980s, Lieserl, the daughter of the famous genius, donated 1,400 letters, written by Einstein, to the Hebrew University, with orders not to publish their contents until two decades after his death. This is one of them, for Lieserl Einstein.

..."When I proposed the theory of relativity, very few understood me, and what I will reveal now to transmit to mankind will also collide with the misunderstanding and prejudice in the world.

I ask you to guard the letters as long as necessary, years, decades, until society is advanced enough to accept what I will explain below.

There is an extremely powerful force that, so far, science has not found a formal explanation to. It is a force that includes and governs all others, and is even behind any phenomenon operating in the universe and has not yet been identified by us.

This universal force is LOVE.

When scientists looked for a unified theory of the universe they forgot the most powerful unseen force.

Love is Light, that enlightens those who give and receive it.

Love is gravity, because it makes some people feel attracted to others.

Love is power, because it multiplies the best we have, and allows humanity not to be extinguished in their blind selfishness. Love unfolds and reveals.

For love we live and die.

Love is God and God is Love.

This force explains everything and gives meaning to life. This is the variable that we have ignored for too long, maybe because we are afraid of love because it is the only energy in the universe that man has not learned to drive at will.

To give visibility to love, I made a simple substitution in my most famous equation.

If instead of $E=mc^2$, we accept that the energy to heal the world can be obtained through love multiplied by the speed of light squared, we arrive at the conclusion that love is the most powerful force there is, because it has no limits. After the failure of humanity in the use and control of the other forces of the universe that have turned against us, it is urgent that we nourish ourselves with another kind of energy...

If we want our species to survive, if we are to find meaning in life, if we want to save the world and every sentient being that inhabits it, love is the one and only answer. Perhaps we are not yet ready to make a bomb of love, a device powerful enough to entirely destroy the hate, selfishness and greed that devastate the planet.

However, each individual carries within them a small but powerful generator of love whose energy is waiting to be released. When we learn to give and receive this universal energy, dear Lieserl, we will have affirmed that love conquers all, is able to transcend everything and anything, because love is the quintessence of life.

I deeply regret not having been able to express what is in my heart, which has quietly beaten for you all my life. Maybe it's too late to apologize, but as time is relative, I need to tell you that I love you and thanks to you I have reached the ultimate answer! ".

Your father Albert Einstein.

Albert Einstein was a German-born theoretical physicist who developed the theory of relativity, one of the two pillars of modern physics. His work is also known for its influence on the philosophy of science.

Eating Chocolates...
by Anita Moorjani

The meaning of life? In other words, "Why are we here"? To eat chocolate, of course! Why else? ☺

I know you think I'm kidding, but I'm actually not. Well.....ok, we're also here to watch glorious sunsets, to make love with our beloved, to laugh heartily, to love fearlessly, to live life fully and with abandon, and to do all the things that bring us joy.

So if it's really that simple, then why are so many of us living joyless lives? I believe it's because we make it more complicated than it needs to be. Most of us, myself included, have at one time or another, bought into beliefs that tell us we need to do more, be more, work harder, be better. We buy into the fear that we're not good enough the way we are and we need to do whatever it takes to get ahead of everyone else because there isn't enough to go around. So we get on this treadmill, constantly trying to get ahead of the person in front of us. Except the person in front of us is doing exactly the same thing, trying to get ahead of the person in front of *them*!

Ironically, many of us are like that even in our spiritual practices, believing that spirituality needs to be *pursued*, and we need to work at it harder, meditate longer, or read more, to be more spiritual than the next person! Like there isn't enough spirituality to go around! LOL! That kind of spiritual belief is driven by fear, not love. Fear of not being spiritual enough, as opposed to a knowing that we already are spiritual beings, whether we realize it or not, and that we already are everything we are trying to attain.

It wasn't until I *died* that I understood this. I was suffering from what should have been the final stages of lymphatic cancer, when my organs shut down and I went into a coma. I was at death's door, and the doctors told my family that I wasn't coming back. However, while in the coma, I experienced what I would call an "awakening"—also called a "near death experience". During this state, I realized that I had my priorities wrong and had spent a lifetime trying to be something that I'm not.

Death made me revaluate what is actually important in life. When we don't realize this—that death is the ultimate leveler—our priorities are very different. But once we have a glimpse of it and actually experience it and bring that feeling back with us, we realize: *Wow! All these things that I thought mattered actually have no significance on the other side!* It rearranges all our priorities in life—how we live, how we deal with our emotions, everything.

Having already faced death, I now know that spending a lifetime of always playing it safe, for example, by choosing the safest career, by pleasing people, worrying about what everyone else thinks of me, meeting everyone else's expectations except my own, being what everyone else wanted me to be, etc. felt like a totally wasted life. I feel so blessed to have been given a second chance, because most people don't get to come back when they learn that lesson. This time, I plan to pursue my dreams, love more, laugh more, not take life so seriously, and live fearlessly.

Our life is our prayer. It's our gift to the universe. We owe to ourselves and everyone around us to be happy and spread that joy around.

Chocolates, anyone? ☺

❧🍎🍃❧

Anita Moorjani, a New York Times best-selling author of the book *Dying to be Me*, and a world-renowned international speaker, doctors had given her mere hours to live on the morning of February 2, 2006. Unable to move, and in a deep coma caused by the cancer that had ravaged her body for nearly four years, Anita tells of entering another realm where she experienced great clarity and understanding of her life and purpose here on earth. In that realm, she was given a choice of whether to return to life or continue on into death. Anita chose to return to this life when she realized that "heaven" is a state, not a place. This awareness

subsequently resulted in a remarkable and complete recovery of her health within weeks of coming out of the coma.
www.AnitaMoorjani.com

Love is Who We Already Are
by Yogi Amrit Desai

We are born *beings* exploring what life means as *humans*. The ego-mind continually seeks the meaning of life in the dimension of time and space, but we are also born with a divine potential that exists in the timeless zone. This is the true Self, the soul that we are.

The ego-mind lives within the limitations of its self-image and self-concepts. It seeks meaning through acquiring and achieving on the material plane. It is a warehouse of memories, storing the dualities of success and failure, ecstasy and agony, pleasure and pain. The meaning of life is measured by increments from the past. Pleasure, happiness, and fulfillment equals success versus pain, misery and disappointment which adds up to failure.

Mired in the self-image, we believe that love, joy and satisfaction come from outside ourselves. Memories of the past plague us and create division and conflict. Our quest invariably fails as long as we remain stuck in our own self-concepts of what the true meaning of life represents.

What appears to be coming from another, either acceptance or rejection, is like the reflection of the moon in a pond. It is an illusion created by the projection of memories, the masking of the present by the past. In our reactive perception, what appears to be present is not real. Just as the ego-mind believes the reflection of the moon to be real, so too, love coming from external relationships is a mirage. The question remains: how skillful a diver do we believe we are to find the moon in the water?

Receiving love from another can never replace the experience of love that comes from the hidden source that resides within. When we seek love from another, the feeling that exists within each of us is replaced with feelings *about* love. *Feelings*, good or bad, are emotionally generated experiences from the past. They are the same illusory reflections of projections, distortions and reactions.

Searching for the meaning of life through the ego-mind is an endless journey through time and space. The meaning of life can never be discovered with the ego-mind that is separated from the source of oneness that is love within.

Love is who we already are.

Reconnecting to the source within is the meaning of life. This inborn urge to merge with the Divine is the fulfillment of the longing of the soul. Only when we realize that the Self *beyond* the self-image is our true self can we access the being beyond the human form that is our destiny.

Yogi Amrit Desai is a world-renowned yoga master and teacher of holistic living, who melds ancient wisdom with modern adaptability. His piercing insight into the nature of life is a road map to fulfillment. Yogi Desai is the creator of Kripalu Yoga and the founder of the Kripalu Center for Yoga and Health. At age 83, he lives and teaches at the Amrit Yoga Institute in Salt Springs, Florida.
www.AmritYoga.org

The Gift of Unconditional Love
By Suzanne Giesemann

The answer to *'what is the meaning of life'* is simple: You as a soul have temporarily taken on human form to develop your divinity. God ... Spirit ... the Divine is Love, therefore you are here to be the presence of Love.

Love is the Force that breathes you. Love is your very essence. It is the Light that burns eternally within you. The brighter that Light shines through your conscious thoughts and actions, the more you are living on purpose.

Ego is associated with the human side of you. The soul is eternal. Ego focuses mainly on the self and sees itself as separate from all others. The soul focuses on unity and our interconnectedness. For most human beings, ego is the default position. The spiritual path, therefore, is the journey from identifying with the ego to identifying with the spirit.

All of the verifiable evidence that has come through in my work as an evidential medium and in meditative communion with the unseen realm has proven to me that we are not the separate beings our egos would like us to believe we are. We are intricately interconnected, and the energy that binds us is the highest of all vibrations: Love.

As Spirit-beings temporarily wearing human suits, it's easy to forget that our essential nature is pure love. It takes a conscious effort to rise above the ego. Life can be one of peace and joy when you realize that your purpose is to express your Divinity and you then live every moment fulfilling that purpose.

A meaningful, love-centered life is one in which you give no power to fear, anger, or judgment, but see every encounter and every event as an opportunity to respond with love. As a love-centered person, you deliberately focus on setting ego aside and living as a fully-realized spirit. Peace comes when you stop seeking outside of yourself for love and realize that the love you seek is right there at your center. The more you express your true Self through the gift of your unconditional love, the more your life has meaning.

❧❀❧

Suzanne Giesemann is the author of eleven books, a metaphysical teacher, and an evidential medium. Suzanne's gift of communication with those on the other side provides stunning evidence of life after death. Suzanne is a retired U.S. Navy Commander. She served as a commanding officer, as special assistant to the Chief of Naval Operations, and as Aide to the Chairman of the Joint Chiefs of Staff on 9/11. Today Suzanne addresses questions about the purpose of life, the nature of reality, and attuning to higher consciousness. Her work has been recognized as highly credible by afterlife researcher Dr. Gary Schwartz, Ph.D., and best-selling author Dr. Wayne Dyer. She is a member of the Advisory Council of the Academy for Spiritual and Consciousness Studies, and she serves on the Executive Council of Eternea, where she is also the Chairman of the Spirituality Leadership Council. www.SuzanneGiesemann.com

THAT Which We Are
by Pace Freeborn

Love, joy, happiness, trust, compassion, expansion, spiritual evolution... these are but I few things that rise within when thinking about the meaning of life. What more can there be to life than to be happy, to play and to laugh, to extend compassion to another, to serve and to evolve?

It's so easy to get caught up on the things of the world and we lose sight of what really matters, and that is to come home to your Self, to find out that in the midst of chaos we are the One that is observing it all playing out before us, like a scene in a movie. We are the Impersonal Observer that is here to enjoy the smell of the freshly cut grass, the taste of grandma's apple pie, the sight of the most majestic sunrise, the sound of the birds singing along with each other, and the feeling of the sand between our toes.

It's to experience life. To experience the love of another and to experience the pain. It's to dance all night long and to pursue our passions that rise from within. And it's so expand and to evolve, coming home to the Impersonal Observer, the Source within, and to see that all along we are abiding in heaven, dancing with the angels and with all those that have come before us and those that have yet to come. It's to experience our very nature, our Natural State of Being of love, joy, peace, patience, kindness, goodness, gentleness, faithfulness, and self-control. And it is to offer up all of our resistance so that we may be THAT WHICH WE ARE, unmovable, unshakable, resting in All That Is.

Circumstances in life come and go. Lessons are learned and, through that, we expand into a fuller expression of our Truth. How beautiful it is to come to understand that each circumstance, every pain, hurt, rejection, joy, praise, blessings are all Grace; a most auspicious gift from God that is offered to us as a token along the path home, communicating to us that we are never alone. When we awaken to this we see that each moment of our lives, this one and the next, has been perfectly laid out, giving meaning to each moment, every minute of every day. And we come to see that our very existence is here, Now, and the only offering for us to give in our complete surrender to the Source of All That Is. In this, we see the sunrise, hear the birds sing, taste grandma's apple pie, feel the sand between our toes, and smell the freshly cut grass as though for the first time, every time.

Oh, and one last thing! It's to realize the miracle it is that you are *alive!* A spirit in human form that gets to experience all of this! Wow! Can there be any better that to simply be the Experiencer?

Ah! The meaning of life. Laughing. Dancing. Experiencing. Expanding. Evolving. Coming Home! Oh the joy in coming home!

Pace Freeborn is a spiritual teacher, writer, and soon to be author on Inner Transformation and Awakening.

"Words cannot begin to describe the passion and love within. Nor can words adequately describe that which I AM. I am Life. I am Love. I am Light. I am that which you are. An extension of Source, a being of God. Some would call that a mystic. I call that Truth."

Please click the link below to learn more about Pace, their awakening, and a little about how the pain from the past was the catalyst of Grace to launch them into the arms of their Inner Being. www.PaceFreeborn.ca

Bowing to the Sacredness of Life
by Nubia Teixeira

The meaning of life to me is to love.

Learning how to love fully is a big part of our journey as humans. Learning how to love can become our whole spiritual path, and although all that you need for that practice is already inside, it's not so easy to surrender to that power within oneself. The deeper you walk into its inner sanctum's light, the more blind you feel.

How "loving" manifests in this physical reality it is not black or white, it is not conventional, it doesn't follow a specific tradition, it doesn't belong to one person's point of view. Loving is unconditional, universal and all-embracing. Love (and loving) has so many different facets, cultures, creeds, and colors and it reflects a wide spectrum of existence. The exercise of loving starts with "learning to love oneself fully". This might be a lifetime voyage, with lots of ups and downs, twists and turns.

When graduating in the skill of loving oneself, one must upgrade to a whole other level of challenge: "learning how to love another (and others) fully", without restrictions, blaming, comparing or judging – unconditionally loving others as you deepen in your relationships and accept the beautiful uniqueness of all beings.

This might grant to a sincere practitioner a "master's degree" in loving, and that knowledge might propel a devotee to embark on a worldwide study of "learning how to love all and see all as spiritual beings in material bodies".

Ultimately, learning to love and take care of this benevolent planet is one of the main needs of our time and age. When we, through the eyes of love, can perceive our physical body and the body of the Earth as one, love and caring will take on a new meaning. Everyone will find, in their own way, and in their own time, a riverine stream that will guide them as individuals to the big ocean of Oneness.

I have found that, for me, the path of Bhakti Yoga has given me tools to channel all my feelings, emotions and challenges towards the ONE BIG HEART that BIG BANGS me down to my knees over and over again, bowing to the sacredness in my heart and to the sacredness of life.

Om Love Om

❧⁂☙

Nubia Teixeira, a Brazilian born yogini, Nubia has been devoting herself to teaching Yoga, in its many different aspects, for the past 25 years. Perceiving Yoga as a healing art, her refinement and connection to this ancient practice is reflected in her unique teaching style. Adorning her Yoga teaching with the symbology of Odissi, Nubia

infuses elements of sacred geometry and devotion of this classical dance form in her offerings. Rooted in her decades of training and embodiment of these traditions, Nubia bridges the ancient into the modern. She is the author of the instructional CD: *Pranayama; May our Breath be our Prayer.* Nubia teaches locally in Marin, California and world wide with her husband Jai Uttal.
www.BhaktiNova.com

What is the Meaning of Life?
by Eben Alexander

Elucidating the "Meaning of Life" can best be approached through application of the ancient directive: "Know yourself." To fathom the depths of this suggestion, it helps to view the boundaries of self as false and misleading. The physical universe is a small subset of the much grander aspects of the spiritual universe, of which we are all a part. And, more than just a part, in a holographic sense, our conscious existence is a crucial aspect of all existence, ultimately identical with all of the universe.

There is one consciousness of which all life is an integral part, and it is the fundamental substrate out of which emerges everything else in all of existence. Each of us is as a holographic reflection of the entire self-aware universe, unlimited in our capabilities. The entire universe exists to serve as the stage on which the drama of sentient life unfolds, and we each participate in that much grander process, that in its most robust form is the "evolution of consciousness" about which Pierre Teilhard de Chardin so eloquently wrote.

In some sense, labeling this realm "soul school" emphasizes that existence is all about learning, and teaching. We are all participants, but it makes more sense to take the broadest view possible—to see all of the participating souls and soul groups, and all of their trials and tribulations, to be the course material for this grand process of understanding, of coming to "know oneself."

Much of the confusion in our attempts to understand existence arises from our false sense of separation, from analyzing a small portion of the universe (i.e. ourselves) as independent from the universe. Such false separation leads to confusion and distortion. It is much better to take the broadest view possible—of our soul groups' members over many incarnations, to view all of our human interactions and relationships as a meaningful construct of learning and teaching— with the core currency of those lessons steeped in Love as the common denominator.

The ultimate "meaning" thus emerges from this process of learning and teaching, of finding that the ultimate moral compass in our efforts is the most ideal application of unconditional love, compassion, forgiveness, acceptance and mercy – for ourselves, our neighbors, our "enemies," indeed for all fellow beings throughout creation. This unconditional love has infinite power to heal, whether the healing involves the individual, the soul group, or much larger groups of sentient life throughout the cosmos. The microcosm of existence in each of our lives is thus reflected as the *raison d'être* for the entirety of existence.

Eben Alexander III MD

After decades as a physician and teacher at Harvard Medical School and elsewhere, renowned academic neurosurgeon Dr. Eben Alexander thought he knew how the brain, mind, and consciousness worked. A transcendental Near-Death Experience (NDE) during a week-long coma from an inexplicable brain infection changed all of that – completely. Memories of his life had been completely deleted, yet he awoke with memories of a fantastic odyssey deep into another realm – more real than this earthly one!

His most recent book, *Living in a Mindful Universe: A Neurosurgeon's Journey into the Heart of Consciousness*, (co-authored with Karen Newell) has garnered accolades from many scientists around the world who study the mind-body question and the nature of consciousness. His earlier books, *Proof of Heaven: A Neurosurgeon's Journey into the Afterlife* and *The Map of Heaven: How Science, Religion, and Ordinary People Are Proving the Afterlife*, have collectively spent more than two years atop the New York Times and international bestseller lists. www.EbenAlexander.com

Love and Acceptance
by Chris Shelton

Two words sums up the meaning of life: *Love and Acceptance.*

I believe that Love is all there is, and that Love heals. I'm not just talking about romantic love but Universal Love. The type of Love that has no opposite. The type of Love that heals and transforms.

We find peace through acceptance (non-resistance) when we allow the events of life to unfold easily and naturally. Acceptance is a state of allowing, loving, believing. An overriding belief that All is Well and that life is happening *for* us and not *to* us.

Most people think that acceptance means giving up, being weak or passive, not showing up or quitting when the going gets tough. Quite the contrary. Living from a place of acceptance demonstrates great inner strength. It's a powerful act of letting go of control... and we love to feel in control. We've been taught that if we are in control and command of our lives, we are safe, secure and comfortable. But control demands control over others and that's where madness and fear can overshadow Love and Acceptance.

Without Acceptance, we miss opportunities to transform situations into outcomes that benefit all of us. When illness and dis-ease enter, we are especially susceptible to the trickery of shadow. Fear always invites us to get stuck and stay stuck in rigid mind patterns that distort Love and Acceptance.

Pain and suffering is the great equalizer and great teacher. Suffering always asks: Who are you?

There was a time in my life when I felt tremendous anger towards what I perceived as the unfairness of life. I felt victimized by an accident that left me partially paralyzed. A childhood that wasn't perfect. A marriage that didn't work out. Looking back, I feel such Love and gratitude for that fearful young man. Pain and suffering was the great alchemist because once everything was burned away, I had the inner space and quiet to study Qigong, Chinese Medicine and Taoist philosophy. These traditions showed me what life could look like when I approached life with an open heart rather than a closed mind and clenched fist.

Qigong taught me Love and Acceptance.

I believe part of our destiny as humans is to learn, transform and evolve. Many of us believe that our fate is written in stone or spiraled into our DNA. I'm here to say that's not correct thinking. From misfortune and heartache comes the potential for deep, everlasting awakening that can change your fate/destiny/life path. When we learn from our experiences, we gain wisdom. We become kinder and wiser.

As we honor our divine nature, we access greater sources of Love and Acceptance, and the feeling that All is Well. My life is deeper and more meaningful when I make the conscious choice to see everything – and everyone – as independent from the low-energy labels of good, bad, right, wrong.

Everything just *is*. Approaching life with Love and Acceptance make that truth easier to live and blesses us with a life that's joyful and hopeful, too.

❧❦❧

Chris Shelton is a certified practitioner and teacher with 15 years of clinical experience in Qigong. Chris' belief in the healing powers of Qigong is rooted in first-hand experience. As a teenager he suffered from a devastating back injury that left him in constant pain and partially paralyzed. He attributes his full recovery to Qigong, a holistic approach perfect for people who want non-invasive, affordable and empowering healthcare. He is founder of Morning Crane Healing Arts Center in San Jose, California, and the author of *Qigong for Self-Refinement* and host of YouTube series 30 Days Qigong to Better Health. www.SheltonQiGong.com

Life is... like a star, or the sky, or the field of orchids
by Laura Plumb

What is the meaning of life?

I once heard Joseph Campbell answer this question by saying he doesn't believe there is so much *a meaning to life*, but rather that we are alive to feel ourselves fully alive, and that when we come fully alive we feel that our lives are meaningful.

After all, what is the meaning of birds singing, or the wind blowing, or trees swaying in that wind, or mountains reaching to the sky, or flowers whose faces turn to follow the sun over the course of a day?

I guess the meaning is that we are alive and it means something to have a life. It means you get to see those things, feel, smell, touch and listen. It means you get to have experiences that move, excite, rub, imprint, hurt, uplift, awaken, enlighten...

Maybe it means we get to love even when love feels like the last worst option, or attune ourselves to see rays of light in the darkest places, or we get to wake up even when the day seems impossible... Cumulatively this would give meaning. Your life would hold the meaning of presence, or the meaning of integrity, or dignity, or commitment.

Primarily life *is*. It's a verb, not a book, or a philosophy or a star spangled meaning. Life just *is* – like a star *is*, or the sky *is*, or the field of orchids growing behind a waterfall that are rarely seen and yet rise to the sky in a silent exaltation of beauty. What is the meaning of that?

Like Camus, I believe that life has inherent worth even if it doesn't have a meaning. So maybe that is it – we are here to grow and bloom and rise up towards heaven, and do it, not to be seen, not for external value, but because *you are alive to be the coming alive of you*: exalted, beautiful and worthy.

🐾🐾

Laura Plumb is the the best-selling author of *Ayurveda Cooking For Beginners*, the writer and host of a 53-part tv series called *VedaCleanse* and a 12-part series called *Divine Yoga*. Laura is a leading educator on the power of the Vedic sciences to promote sacred, sumptuous living. Formerly the General Manager of The Discovery Channel Europe, Laura is the founder/director of VedaWise, offering clinical services in natural medicine for whole person wellness and trainings in the Vedic sciences.
www.LauraPlumb.com
www.food-alovestory.com

The Creator's Breath... a Reflection of Love
by Steven Weiss

Hmmm... Love... is the meaning of Life?

As my thoughts begin unwinding along the Path that these words take me... I must first ask myself, "what do I mean by **Love**?"

Whew!

Love... **Love!** My mind struggles a bit to wrap around a meaning that might reside behind this word! However, despite my mind's workings, I feel my heart open with the sense of Love; a warmth; a joy. Perhaps this is a clue? I recall a passage from a book I read somewhere that offered the idea that love is that which we experience when we see the Divine reflected in someone or something. That Love is an *allowing* rather than a *doing*[1]. however at this point my brain shuts down and I realize that I am going to have to come back to Love later. Maybe there will be some clarity later after have gotten somewhat further into this exploration into *love and the meaning of Life*.

"And what do I mean by the word **Meaning**?" I am stuck here too, however I had better push through this or I am lost.

As one who strives to move toward the non-duality of things, is there not meaning in all things? A meaning behind *all* things?

Is there anything which does not have meaning? I hear the words of a woman Apache elder teacher (Shanadii Crosby in New Mexico) who would frequently remind us that "nothing has meaning except for the meaning we give it!" Quickly followed by, "and since all things were Breathed by Creator, how could they not all have meaning... and be perfect just the way they are?"

So a mind seeks meaning... and in doing so creates judgment... and a duality-driven series of barriers or boxes... "this particular thing has meaning on this side... and this other thing does not on the other... this is sacred... and of course this is profane."

However, when I seek meaning... and attach meaning... and create meaning... do I not risk missing the fundamental essence of a thing ("the Tao which can be named is not the Tao"[2])? I miss the possibility of sitting and Being with the thing in and of itself... of getting out of the way a letting it "talk" to me, rather than engaging my mind to analyze it. It feels impossible to be open and Present to a thing... while at the same time analyzing, probing and deconstructing it for its meaning.

("So the pilgrim said, 'I wish to know the meaning of life, father.' And the Dalai Lama smiled and said, 'Well my son, life is like a beanstalk, isn't it?'"[3]...)

Sorry...

And then... for comic relief... my mind keeps remembering the scene in "Conan the Barbarian" in which, when asked by a Mongol General, "What is best in life?" Conan replies, "To crush your enemies, to see them driven before you, and to hear the lamentations of their women."

And then what of the word "Life" itself? What do I mean by Life? Is life a Light, like the sun, that crosses the otherwise black sky of death (non-life)? Or, as Huang Po, the 6th Patriarch of Chinese Buddhism (9th century) (also striving to achieve the non-duality behind all phenomena, teachings, and practices) emphasizes... the sky is the same sky whether the sun is traveling across it... or the moon... or whether it is in total darkness... That the light and dark are merely varying expressions of the same Thing (which does not change depending upon whether it is expressed as light or darkness!).

So back to an old teaching about how life and death are both expressions of the same thing... that the greater part of us is non-physical and eternal... whether manifesting in a body or not.

So... when I say Life... am I referring to the eternal cycle of life and death (where we never die and all is life)... or just that part of the life/death dance in which we inhabit a physical body? And where... and how... do I find meaning in that?

I just read an article about the recent discovery of an observable strong flash of fluorescent light emitted the instant that a sperm fertilizes an egg (apparently caused by surges of calcium and zinc)... perhaps evidence of what mystical traditions have long described as the Spark of Life, though, traditionally, other teachings talk about the Spark of Life as the moment when Creator Breathes a soul... which will then incarnate as a physical being....

However... all things are Breathed by Creator...

And as we are all Breathed we are all filled with Light in one instant... only later to Breathe out and diminish in Light in the next... in a tidal waveform of a rising and receding tide... where that "intertidal zone" of this tide is where Life is expressed.

(The Huna of Hawaii teach that when we are born we borrow Creator's Breath (and the life that comes with it) with the in-breath of HA... and at the moment of our passing we give back the borrowed Creator's Breath with a final HA exhalation...)

I like that by now in this exploration (regardless of any personal meaning that I might have derived from it) I am sitting... *just sitting*... with Creator's Breath... and Creation... and have defied the drive of my finite little brain (in search of Meaning) to turn over all the stones around me on the beach where I find myself sitting... within a vast Stillness... while the tide and waves continue to rise and fall around and within me. And in this state of Breath... and Tide... I feel the Spirit of the natural world being Breathed... the Breath that flows though exquisite music... the first Breath of a newborn baby... the touch of the Beloved's skin... the Stillness behind and beyond all things.

And quite irrationally I am suddenly and deeply aware that the *substance* of the Stillness, Creator's Breath, the tide that rises and falls before me and the very *composition* of this Divine water and air, and in fact the glue that holds together all Creation... is a reflection of Love.

How could be otherwise?

I am not sure that I can speak much about the meaning of life... or love. however, in this moment... in this state... I can say that here... in this "place"... Life has meaning for me... and all around and within me is Love.

1. Stubbs, Tony, *An Ascension Handbook*, World Tree Press, 1992, pp. 61-65
2. Lao Tzu, *Tao Te Ching*, translated by Jane English and Gia-Fu Feng, Vintage Press, 1997
3. Lyrics from an old Procol Harum song)

Dr. Steven Weiss is a licensed osteopathic physician, board certified in the specialty practice of "Neuro-musculoskeletal Osteopathic Manipulative Medicine." He consults in the fields of chronic pain, sports and performing arts medicine, and the treatment of prenatal and pediatric problems. As stated above, for nearly 30 years he has devoted his career to pursuing and applying those clinical/healing approaches that invoke and support the power of the human body to heal and regulate itself! He is internationally recognized for his clinical success — an uncanny ability to help people suffering from complex and seemingly unsolvable clinical problems.

Dr. Weiss is the Medical Director of the Medicine Lodge Clinic, and the founder and educational director of The Altar of Creation Curriculum professional training program for health care practitioners.
www.TheMedicineLodgeClinic.com

Animals and Unconditional Love
by Tim Link

Oh, yes, the age-old question that haunts us on a daily basis. What is the meaning of life? Why am I here? Do I have a purpose, and if so, what is that purpose?

We have all pondered this question and continue to search for the answer far and wide. We often go on religious, spiritual or shamanic journeys in an attempt to find the answer. We seek the advice of the elderly who have lived long enough to have seen it all. We seek the advice of scholars, teachers and enlightened masters. We read "new age" and "self-help" books to try to figure it all out. However, for most of us, including the so-called experts, it continues to be an elusive and sometimes futile journey.

We are all taught by our parents to study diligently in school, get good grades, graduate, get a good job and work hard to "make it" in this world. We try to follow their direction, go to school, get the good grades, the good job, work hard, start a family and climb the corporate ladder. However, somewhere near the top of the ladder we stop and ask ourselves the burning questions, "Is this it?" "Is this all there is to life?"

We spend a good portion of our life pondering these questions. For some, we spend most of our life and perhaps thousands of dollars in therapy in order to attempt to understand just a small sliver of what it is all about.

We all have a purpose in life. Every living being, human or animal, selects a body or host when we come into this world. We are here to fulfill a specific purpose in this life. Some are teachers and some are healers. Some are caretakers and some need to be taken care of. Some are leaders and some are followers. Whatever the purpose is, no matter how grandiose or simple it may seem, we are all here for a purpose. Trying to figure out that purpose seems to be the most challenging thing for most of us. We always think the answers are somewhere outside of ourselves or that someone else has all the answers. When in truth, the answer lies within each of us. The answers have been with us all along. We just need to slow down, breathe and let it flow.

I do believe animals have the best grasp on the real meaning of life. They understand their purpose and try to fulfill their purpose each and every day. They work diligently and are always willing to share their purpose with us. They fulfill that purpose until they feel they have completed their purpose or their bodies no longer will support them and they move on.

Animals are just like their human companions. Some our teachers and some are healers. Some are caretakers and some need to be taken care of. Some are leaders and some are followers. The only difference is that they apply themselves to fulfilling their purpose every day and try not to let anyone or anything detour them from it.

The biggest example of this is an animal's ability to provide unconditional love. They are always willing to provide love to their human companions and those around them. No matter their past, they live in the present and realize that unconditional love is the reason we are all here. Without unconditional love none of us can realize, let alone fulfill, our own life's purpose.

So, at the end of the day we should all be asking ourselves, "What is the meaning of life?" The answer should come through loud and clear. It is unconditional love for everyone and everything around us. Unconditional love is the answer.

⁂

Tim Link
–is the best-selling author of *Talking with Dogs* and *Cats and Wagging Tales: Every Animal Has a Tale*
–is the host of the Animal Writes show on Pet Life Radio and iHeartRadio

–is a regular contributing writer for Victoria Stilwell's Positively, Species Link and Dogster and Catster magazines

–has been featured in publications including The Associated Press, The Atlanta Journal-Constitution, People magazine's People Pets, Gwyneth Paltrow's goop magazine

–has been a featured guest on many radio stations including WSB, NPR, Sirius XM Shirley MacLaine's "Independent Expression" show

–has appeared on every major US Network

–has professionally recorded several audio meditations and audio workshops that are available through iTunes, Amazon and CD Baby.

www.wagging-tales.com

The Purpose of Life... is to Love
by Howard Martin

I believe the meaning of life is to express love. That is a rather broad statement. Let me explain what I mean.

Love is a little word that covers a lot of territory. It can be seen as something to avoid by some, the unifying force behind all of creation by others and a lot in between. In essence it is hard to define.

We experience it as a strong feeling that most often cannot be captured in words. For example, the love we have when we are in the early stages of romance has an amazing, up-lifting, regenerative quality that is hard to describe or explain. The deep love we can have for our children and family has a connection and a power that evokes the highest levels of care and self-sacrifice for the well-being of others. That kind of love is not easily described either. The love of life and our desire to preserve it even when it can seem miserable cannot be fully explained by words alone. Even though love cannot be fully defined it is the one thing we all want.

Pondering the meaning of life always leads me to wanting to better understand the reality of love. My exploration has led to one thing I believe.

I believe the purpose of life, what gives life meaning, is to love.

I know that statement could seem lofty, idealistic and out of touch. We live in a world that is often hard, cold, unforgiving and full of misery and pain.

Painful personal, societal and global issues are certainly real but somehow, some way, despite all of the hardships, humanity has expressed such beauty and intelligence. I believe it is through the power of love that this occurs. For the people who have very little or ones that have significant issues and challenges, it is the love they feel, however fleeting that gets them through. The love they feel from their families, the acts of kindness they experience from time to time, the feeling they have when nature displays its intricate beauty is what makes life worth living. The wonder of life, the love people have for life somehow provides the impetus to keep growing and trying.

Love, in all it's forms, is what gives life it's deeper meaning.

Most importantly I believe this. When my life here comes to an end and I transition from this version of reality to another, the measure of how I lived, what I accomplished, what I left behind and what it has meant will be based simply on how much I loved. That is what will really matter. That is my meaning, my purpose.

Howard Martin is an author, speaker, trainer and musician. He is the Executive Vice President at HeartMath.
www.HeartMath.com

The Journey of Love
by Karen Wyatt

In my work as a hospice medical director I have spent a lot of time thinking and talking about the meaning of life. On many occasions I have sat at the bedside of a dying patient and contemplated that very question: "What is life all about?" Of course, in those instances we were looking at life in retrospect, taking one person's life as a whole, with all of its ups and downs, and trying to understand what it all had meant.

I have learned that the meaning of life is actually much easier to grasp from the vantage point of one's last days on Earth than at any previous time of life. During earlier stages of existence, life is complex and confusing with jobs and housework and community commitments and politics and religion and relationships all competing for attention — all creating their own sense of meaning and purpose. But when death is near, everything superficial has been stripped away; everything that dragged us into the past or pushed us into the future has disappeared; everything that required time and effort has been discarded. Then the true meaning of this existence can be seen shining and illuminating the present moment.

Each time I have accompanied a patient on this search for meaning, one common thread has emerged: that life, a tapestry of beauty and pain, accomplishment and failure, clarity and confusion, is really a journey of love; that learning all the intricacies and nuances of love itself is the reason we came here; that the greatest gift of life is the opportunity to give, receive and become love.

I believe that we are Spirits who have materialized into physical form in order to witness the diversity, expanse and creativity of love as it courses through, to, from and between us. If we can fix our gaze on nothing other than love during this lifetime, then we will have discovered the deepest possible meaning life has to offer. It is so simple and yet so difficult for us to grasp this reality and to allow love to guide our lives. But following the path that love unfolds before us is truly the key to finding life's meaning.

❦❧

Karen Wyatt MD is a hospice and family physician and the author. She is a frequent keynote speaker and radio show guest whose profound teachings have helped many find their way through the difficult times of life. Dr. Wyatt received the Spirit of the American Woman Award in 1996, was named one of Utah's 100 Notable Women in that same year, and in 2005 was a recipient of the Outstanding Citizen of the Year Award for Summit County, Colorado.
www.KarenWyattMD.com

The Experience of True Love
By Satyanarayana Dasa

Every living being has an inherent nature to avoid pain and to attain happiness. This nature is most developed in human beings. Whatever we do in our life, knowingly or unknowingly, we do so with the intention to be happy and not to suffer. There are various ways to attain happiness but the greatest happiness which we can experience comes from love. When love is there, there is only happiness and life has deep meaning. Without love we may have various experiences of pleasure, yet they are fleeting.

Inevitably each time we come down from a pleasurable experience, our life appears incomplete because we are facing the very pain we have been trying to avoid. Basically our drive in our life is only for love, and so we go on seeking more pleasurable temporary experiences. But we do not stop to ask why am I not happy? Most people continue to seek love where it does not exist such as in wealth, power, position, name, sex, drugs, and fame. All these look very appealing, but ultimately, they don't bring the satisfaction which comes from true love. Unfortunately, most people do not have the experience of pure unconditional true love.

True love is possible only between two living beings and not between a living being and an insentient object, like wealth. True love is a steady state, meaning that you can not come down from it. Once you have it, you are in that state eternally. This is in contrast to romantic love, where you fall in love and out of love.

But, to have an experience of true love, it is not so easy. You first have to understand your own true self. Who are you? Who are you beyond your roles, titles, and accomplishments in life? How do you define yourself, when all else fades away? What still remains? In our conditioned state we identify with our mind and body and so we think we are that. We think we are the mother, or father, or husband or wife, or marketing executive, or teacher, or engineer or doctor. Then we seek love at the level of body and mind, falling in love with the other person's title or role, instead of seeking love at the level of the soul – the unchanging part of a person.

Basically, there are two ways we can derive happiness. One is by being self-centered such as trying to gratify our own senses physically or mentally, which is what happens in a typical romantic relationship. Ultimately this love of the body and mind leads to frustration and instability because your love vacillates just as your body and mind are constantly changing.

The other type of happiness is called love-centered in which the center is not "I" but the object of love. The basic principle of true love is different. In true love, you live for the happiness of the object of love. Your happiness does not come from if your lover can make you happy, it is the opposite. In true love, your happiness comes from if you can make your object of love happy. Your whole focus is on pleasing your love. By giving happiness to the object of love, the lover feels happy naturally and there is not a limit to this happiness. This is the real meaning of life.

❧

Sri Satyanarayana Dasa Babaji was drawn to spiritual traditions of his home country India since childhood. After receiving a postgraduate degree in 1978 from ITT Delhi, he then worked in the United States for four years. After this period, he returned to India to begin formal study of the orthodox systems of Indian philosophy known as sad-darsana under the direct guidance of his guru Sri Haridasa Sastri Maharaja and Svami Syama Sarana Maharaja. This education was pursued in the traditional manner for more than 25 years as he dedicated himself to the practice of bhakti-yoga. In 1991 he accepted the traditional Vaisnava order of renounced life, Babaji-vesa. He also earned four sastric degrees, and received both a law degree and PhD in Sanskrit. Satyanarayana Dasa is the director of the Jiva Institute of Vaishnava Studies in Vrindavan, India.
www.jiva.org

The Feeling of Pure Love
by Karen Newell

Each of us is a unique reflection of a whole and it is our purpose to discover that singular essence within, to remember who we truly are in a grander sense. From there, we are then able to become our full potential, likely more than we can currently imagine. By going deep within our individual consciousness through meditation, introspection or mindfulness practices, we are able to glimpse this larger picture and to feel more readily our connection to the whole.

We are fundamentally spiritual beings who are privileged to temporarily inhabit a human body and we would be wise to cherish such an experience here in the physical realm. When it seems our world is crumbling around us, our response to such challenges is the key to living. Knowing that all adversity has a higher purpose is essential.

Maintaining a sense of grace, acceptance and ease allows us to face our hardships knowing they are part of a larger plan to strengthen both our character and greater soul. This can be accomplished most easily by practicing a demeanor of neutrality and non-judgment towards ourselves and others. We learn best through personal experience and expanding to a wider view helps us to realize our part in this process.

Ultimately, learning to love our self is crucial to life. We are taught the importance of loving others the same as we love our self and indeed, many are focused on helping others. Yet, simultaneously, we are taught that to put our self first is narcissistic and undesirable. In the end, we all are containers of love and need only to activate that love already inside of us. This is accomplished by recalling a feeling of pure love, such as that of a playful puppy.

As we consciously generate that love in our hearts, we actually become the love that we are. Such beneficial feeling causes our heart field to expand widely around the body. The energy of love contained within that heart field then affects others around us, without them necessarily knowing. Through practiced awareness of the heart's field, we can actively expand it through expressions of joy, love and gratitude. The more of us who accomplish this, the more loving our collective world will become.

❧❧❧

Karen Newell

As an innovator in the emerging field of brainwave entrainment audio meditation, Karen Newell, co-founder of Sacred Acoustics, empowers others in their journeys of self-discovery. Using Sacred

Acoustics recordings, she teaches how to connect to inner guidance, achieve inspiration, improve wellness and develop intuition.

In her search for answers to fundamental questions, it became clear that direct experience is crucial to full understanding. To bolster her strong sense of inner knowing and alignment with her higher nature, she enrolled in a series of hands-on experiential courses to investigate and develop such skills as lucid dreaming, astral travel, telepathy, remote viewing, self-hypnosis, and different forms of energy healing.

She is co-author with Dr. Alexander of their latest book, *Living in a Mindful Universe: A Neurosurgeon's Journey into the Heart of Consciousness* (Rodale, 2017). www.SacredAcoustics.com

Love Gives Meaning to Every Breath of Life
by Jennie Lee

Love. Love is the meaning, the purpose, the beginning, and the end of life. It is the harmonizing, unifying energy of the Universe from which we all sprang and to which we all return.

Whether we recognize ourselves as the love that we are, or not, is the critical difference between a life of peace and joy, and a life of stress and sorrow. It is our choice to remember, to re-unite our individualized consciousness with the Divine Source of Love, expanding into an awareness of our loving omniscience.

This is the path of yoga. It is what I teach and try to live each day. Love gives meaning to every breath and the breath is my constant reminder to offer and to receive love every day in every way I can, with each person I encounter, whether we 'like' each other humanly or not.

Through meditation, I have tapped an inner well of love that transcends personal connection. I have realized that as I stay connected to this energy, then all becomes much clearer and I feel guided to the people, places and things I am meant to interact with.

Striving to source every choice, every communication and every action from love, keeps me anchored in the greatest meaning I can imagine for life, and it keeps me connected to pure joy. Love is joyful and so if we bring it full circle I would conclude that the meaning of life is love and the joy that springs from it.

❧❀❧

Jennie Lee is the author of *Breathing Love: Meditation in Action* and *True Yoga: Practicing with the Yoga Sutras for Happiness & Spiritual Fulfillment.* She is a certified Yoga Therapist and spiritual life coach who has been in practice for over 20 years. Jennie counsels clients worldwide, helping them overcome grief, anxiety, and stress, and to create lives of greater joy. Her writing has been featured in dozens of wellness blogs and magazines and she runs wellness retreats internationally. When she is not writing or coaching, she enjoys surfing and hiking with her husband in Hawaii. www.JennieLeeYogaTherapy.com

Life is Meaningless Without Love
by Phil Cousineau

The perennial question about the meaning of life is a riddle posed to us the moment we first become conscious. The very idea of meaning is as puzzling as Winston Churchill's description of Russia as a riddle wrapped in a mystery inside an enigma, and it's risky as the question the Sphinx posed to Oedipus on the road to Delphi. If he doesn't answer her riddle correctly, she purrs, he will die. (He does; she flings herself off a cliff.) The legend suggests that a part of us risks death, figuratively speaking, if we don't at least attempt to answer the great riddles of life, that we cannot pass by the great obstacles set in front of us, we cannot advance, we cannot reach our destination. For it is the attempt that makes us human. This is the function of philosophy, mythology, and art, as most dramatically revealed in riddles, koans, paradoxes, and the Big Questions, such as the meaning of life. They are devised to get us to think for ourselves, and to use our imagination, not to claim authority and most definitely not divine revelation.

For me that is the meaning and the beauty and the numinous power of the question about any so-called meaning of life, which is easy to mock, as the Monty Python movie of the same name does so side-splittingly well, but isn't as easy to explain away. We can laugh but eventually we will find ourselves at some hinged moment when we need to say to decide for ourselves what is important, significant, or has value, which is how meaning reveals — or doesn't — isn't revealed. To say there is no meaning in a moment or an experience by definition means it is "meaningless," which is to say it has no real importance, no significance, no value. Life flattens out and torpor sets in, the psychic numbing that sociologists warn us about, or conversely, we settle for a life of doing only what we want and only for ourselves.

Even so, there will be come a time when life will throttle us and ask if there isn't more. Such is the moment evoked by the Japanese poet Issa, who wrote so sparsely and heartbreakingly, "*And yet , and yet, and yet,*" after the death of his infant daughter, as he yearns for a greater *meaning* beyond the apparent arbitrary nature of her loss.

Not to speculate or ruminate or contemplate the question makes us a little less human, a little more robotic. The best we can do, that reflective people have always done, is to describe rather than define what the question means for ourselves. For me, the meaning of life is two-fold, personal and collective. The collective meaning is what cultures have systematically decided was of *meaning,* which is to say, what has lasting value and a scintilla of truth. Hence, our collections in museums and libraries and now the web are vast repositories of those people believed was of *significance, value, truth*. My growing sense is that art and science are *meaning-making machines*, to coin an expression.

Our art and poetry, inventions and innovations, make visible what is invisible in our hearts and minds. In this sense, meaning is a gleaning, a determining of wisdom out of the glut of information and the Everest of knowledge that we encounter and must climb, and which constantly threatens to overwhelm us. To paraphrase the great Mexican writer, meaning of life is to the need to make things mean, to shake life until it makes sense and reveals its significance, and occasionally gives up, like a mine revealing its veins of gold, a few nuggets of truth.

Essentially, the search for meaning is like the Quest for the Holy Grail, an inner journey for the Grail Knights to the mystery zone of the Grail Castle. The search is a paradox wrapped within a riddle. What is the sound of one mind clapping for meaning? The real work takes place in the heart and mind of lone individuals learning to think for themselves. But the danger lies in devolving into what the Greeks called *omphaloskepsis,* navel-gazing, the practice that drowned Narcissus in the river he gazed into. We did to find our own meaning in order to be awake, alert, and conscious. But that is never enough. The wider and more generous view entails others and the natural world, which is what our most beloved philosophers, artists, mystics, and poets have gone hoarse trying to remind us to do. "I am me plus my circumstances," wrote the Spanish philosopher Jose Ortega y Gasset. My meaning is inextricably connected with the meaning of the world.

That *means,* so to speak, that those involved in the inner realm, our philosophers, in the original sense of the term, those who love wisdom, are our *meaning-makers,* but from two different directions. We go to the historians and journalists and doctors and scientists to find out what happened and when, and then we turn to the poets to speculate on why it matters, or doesn't. In that eternal exchange we discover meaning, what matters, what signifies.

On the philosophical level, which is the realm of meaning, the meaning of life, as in its *purpose,* which is how its is usually explored, comes to one thing, and that is contribution. Life is as meaningful as it involves others, helping, contributing, aiding and abetting, the alternative being trapped in what has recently been called the "youniverse." As in the universe revolves around me, which means in the long run ... nothing. Gazing into our electronic toys is no more gratifying, illuminating, or meaningful than Narcissus gazing at his own reflection in the woodsy pond.

In dramatic contrast is the happiness reported by people the world over by those who live for others, happiness being a kissing cousin of meaningful-ness, as art-making is our most intimate friend. For in the final glimpse, personal meaning isn't the thing to be discovered like some pot of gold at the end of the rainbow, but the thing to *made,* the pot itself, the gold that is melted down. And as Viktor Frankl wrote in his ambrosial book about Auschwitz, *"Challenging* the meaning of life is the truest expression of the state of being human." [my italics] And here is where the question of the meaning of life intersects with the urge to philosophize and to make art. These are our most courageous attempts to deal with our "fractured lives" and the broken lives of others and make sense out of the fragments. T . S . Eliot put it beautifully when we wrote about his own poetry, "These are the fragments I shore against the ruins." Hard-won words that truly reflect our beliefs and the way we lead our lives are the bulwark against the ruins of meaninglessness. In this way, art and philosophy are comparable attempts to *understand everyone's fractures, everyone's brokenness.* Which brings us to one of the most healing thoughts that have survived from antiquity, from the philosopher Philo of Alexandria: "Be kind to everyone you meet because he or she is also enduring a great struggle." Be kind to everyone, including ourselves, because everyone is struggling, day to day, hour to hour, with more than the abstract question of "the meaning of life." They are struggling with the meaning of their own lives and the lives of those around them.

My sense at the beveled edge hour of 3 a.m., when the dark night of the soul gives way to the first light of dawn and reappearance of hope, is that the more we love the question, the more we *love* searching our hearts and the hearts of others who have relished the question, the more we can love life itself. And the more we love, as the great mystics and poets have always reminded us, the less urgent the question is because there is no momentary or ultimate meaning without love, no love without meaning.

I mean the meaning of life is meaningless without love.

***

Phil Cousineau is a writer, teacher, editor, independent scholar, documentary filmmaker, travel leader, and storyteller. His life-long fascination with the art, literature, and history of culture has taken him on many journeys around the world. He lectures frequently on a wide range of topics – from mythology, film, and writing, to beauty, travel, sports, and creativity. He has more than 30 nonfiction books and 15 scriptwriting credits to his name.
www.PhilCousineau.net

Meaning and the Song of the Soul
by Llewellyn Vaughan-Lee

Meaning is what calls from the depths of the soul. It is the song that sings us into life. Whether we have a meaningful life depends upon whether we can hear this song, this primal music of the sacred. The "sacred" is not something primarily religious or even spiritual. It is not a quality we need to learn or to develop. It belongs to the primary nature of all that is. When our ancestors knew that everything they could see was sacred, this was not something taught but instinctively known. It was as natural as sunlight, as necessary as breathing. It is a fundamental recognition of the wonder, beauty and divine nature of the world. And from this sense of the sacred, real meaning is born, the meaning that makes our hearts sing with the deepest purpose of being alive.

Sadly, today so much of life is covered in distractions, in the addictions of consumerism. The soul's music is not easy to hear amidst life's constant clamor, and wonder and mystery have become more and more inaccessible. As a culture we seem to have lost the thread that connects the worlds together: the inner world from which meaning is born, and the outer world where we spend our days. The stories of the soul are no longer told, instead our dreams have become the desires of materialism. Even spirituality is often sold in the marketplace, another drug that promises to placate us, to cover the growing anxiety that something essential is missing.

To find meaning we have to reclaim our sense of the sacred, something our culture appears to have overlooked or forgotten. The sacred is an essential quality of life. It connects us to our own soul and the divine that is the source of all that exists. The sacred can be found in any form: a small stone or a mountain, the first cry of a newborn child and the last gasp of a dying person. It can be present in a loaf of bread, on a table, waiting for a meal, and in the words that bless the meal. The remembrance of the sacred is like a central note within life. Without this remembrance something fundamental to our existence is missing. Our daily life lacks a basic nourishment, a depth of meaning.

When we feel this music, when we sense this song, we are living our natural connection with the Earth and all of life. Meaning is not something that belongs to us, rather our life becomes "meaningful" when we live this connection, when we feel it under our feet as we walk down the street, in the scent of a flower, in rain falling. I am very fortunate in that I live in nature. Early each morning as I walk beside the wetlands—maybe glimpsing an egret, white in the dawn light—I feel this simple connection: how the Earth breathes together with me, how it speaks the language of the soul and of life's mystery. Here meaning is as simple as apple blossoms breaking open, as a young hawk, its feathers still downy, the fog lifting across the water.

We are all part of one living being we call the Earth, magical beyond our understanding. She gives us life and her wonder nourishes us. In her being the worlds come together. Her seeds give us both bread and stories. For centuries the stories of seeds were central to humanity, myths told again and again— stories of rebirth, life recreating itself in the darkness. Now we have almost forgotten these stories. Instead, stranded in our separate, isolated selves we do not even know how hungry we have become. We have to find a way to reconnect with what is essential—to learn once again how to walk in a sacred manner, how to cook with love and prayers, how to give attention to simple things. We need to learn to welcome life in all its colors and fragrances, to say "yes" again and again. Then life will give us back the connection to our own soul, and once more we will hear its song. Then meaning will return as a gift and a promise. And something within our own heart will open and know that we have come home.

❧❧

Llewellyn Vaughan-Lee, Ph.D. is a Sufi mystic and lineage successor in the Naqshbandiyya–Mujaddidiyya Sufi Order. He is an extensive lecturer and author of several books about Sufism, mysticism, dreamwork and spirituality.

His recently published book, *For Love of the Real* (Fall 2015), is regarded as a completion of over twenty-five years of his writing and teaching, as it draws together many of the threads of his work which began with his 1993 book *The Bond with the Beloved*.

www.GoldenSufi.org

Poise in Chaos
by Gloria D. Karpinski

As an intuitive counselor and spiritual teacher for several decades, I can testify the number one question behind all other questions for most people is the quest for meaning. What is the mission? Why am I here? Now?

There is no "one-answer-fits-all" if we speak of appearances on the manifestation level. Everyone's path is a perfect template designed by their soul for individual growth and contribution, from genetics to gender, culture and country, to precise timing of the incarnation. "Know Thyself" written over the Delphic Oracle continues to be the first directive.

Fortunately we have inherited psychological and spiritual therapies, rituals, wisdoms and guidelines from multiple traditions, modern as well as ancient, to help us untie knots that have bound us to illusionary and/or limited concepts of identity and thus our perceptions of purpose.

The deeper we go, the more we seek to understand, the more illusions about who we are *NOT* wither and die as we cease feeding them. We learn to discern the difference between identity and experience. The meaning of life emerges like the sun dissolving a passing cloud cover.

BLESS AND RELEASE is a powerful motto/mantra to incorporate in a daily practice as awareness increases. Using a strong visual image supports a choice to give to one's Highest Self all experiences, biases, pains, anything, everything. An Altar of Light is a strong, simple visual that your subconscious and transcendent will recognize as a place of sacred Offering.

With total honesty about feelings and experience–and willingness to release what is no longer needed–the quest for meaning increasingly becomes one of REMEMBERING that we are quite literally made in the image of the Divine, however we name the Presence. We are incarnated aspects of the One Life, drops of water in the sea of life, incarnated to grow and express in the unique pathways we have chosen and to contribute to the evolutionary pathways of our culture. The intention then becomes one of INTEGRATING "heaven" (in this sense, heaven meaning the awareness of the infinite self) and "earth", our finite physical lives.

Being in the world with intentional pragmatism while staying aware of true identity is a continuing mandate for BALANCING and CREATING with purpose. "Being in the world but not of it." Not one or the other: both/and.

A big aha happens when we realize that as we think, feel, speak and act, we are CREATING realities that will manifest at some point, with or without our awareness. The law of attraction is no more romantic than the law of gravity. The first real encounter with that principle is "Oh, what have I created?" But the power in that recognition can quickly follow as well as its shadow, the seduction of the familiar that has old patterns imprinted in our neurological systems.

In meditation I was guided to *create with care; all things matter. Let go gently; all things pass.*

I once met a Tibetan monk who had been imprisoned and tortured for 21 years. Told I could ask whatever I like, my only question to him was "what got you through it?" He answered that he had not resisted it. *"I embraced it. Because I did, I could practice what I knew."*

Therein is the wisdom. EMBRACE what is present in our lives and we can then use the tools we have and find peace and meaning in the mix of joys and challenges, not as victims but as awake and aware beings. Sometimes we see with clarity how the pieces of our lives reveal purpose; sometimes we see through a mist; and there are passages when we must rely on FAITH that in time all will be revealed.

LOVE is both the ultimate meaning of life and the means, the Way itself. Deeper than the love of personal preferences, unconditional love honors the life force in all of life. It is the alchemy that binds all other elements of awareness together.

PRAYER

I am a Being of Light
Daughter or Son of the Mother Father God
This day only that which is for my Highest
Good shall come to me.
Only that which is Light shall leave from me.

THANK YOU MOTHER-FATHER-GOD

❧🝰🝰

Gloria D. Karpinski is a holistic counselor, spiritual director, teacher and author. Her seminars as well as her individual indepth life attunements emphasize the relevancy of universal spiritual principles to everyday life and the interdynamics of mind, body, emotions and spirit.

She is the author of *Where Two Worlds Touch: Spiritual Rites of Passage* (1991) and *Barefoot on Holy Ground: Twelve Lessons in Spiritual Craftsmanship* (2001).

She is on the advisory board of The Sophia Institute in Charleston, S.C. and a teacher for the Center for Sacred Studies, an international interfaith seminary based in Guerneville, California where her book *Barefoot on Holy Ground* is one of the texts used in the two year seminary program.
www.GloriaKarpinski.com

To Love Everybody
by Peter Sterios

The meaning of life?

Well, it's simple... whenever I am faced with a profound question like this, I seek the advice and wisdom of my most dependable guru, our family's 2-year-old dog, and he never disappoints... For this question his answer was immediate – to love everybody (except maybe the cat next door).

Of course this question has a lot to do with whose life we're referring to. Over 40 years of practicing yoga, I've been aware many times that my point of reference for living in this universe is unique, yet somehow intimately intertwined with every living being on earth – simultaneously a meaningful life is both personal and global. Also, we as a global community have become very human centric and often forget other living beings have perception, have intelligence, and live in ways we cannot normally perceive.

Beyond this planet, I have a deep sense every time I look up into a clear night sky and see stars beyond my imagination expanding infinitely beyond my gaze – that the form of being humans life is likely not the only form of intelligent being. Or similarly, when I turn my gaze inward, and realize the form of being my inner life has is part of an infinite galaxy of cells and subtle body relationships that I have domain over within my ego-based consciousness.

We all are literally swimming in a vast sea of internal and external states of being that miraculously manifest into our individual bodies that have a multitude of experiences on earth to learn and grow from. And exactly why we are here to learn and grow is another mysterious question. Truth is, I'm unclear how to answer that as well. I do know that we all have control over how we relate or react to the entertaining journey our lives experience, full of curiosity, wonder, joy, gratitude, delight, birth, death, sadness, grief, anger, fear, laughter, ecstasy, and love.

In my human experience of being, meaning is greatest when I live a life motivated by love. When I look at other levels of being, (ie galactic or molecular), the definition of love appears to me as bonding, which is essentially the yoga found in nature.

❧ ✿ ❧

Peter Sterios has been part of the global yoga community for over four decades as a teacher, writer, and entrepreneur based in San Luis Obispo, California. He is the creator of Manduka™, an leading eco-yoga products company based in Los Angeles. In 2009, Yoga Journal selected his first DVD, Gravity & Grace in their "top 15 yoga videos of all time". He is an award winning architect, specializing in green yoga studios and retreat centers; co-founder of karmaNICA™, a charitable organization for impoverished kids in western Nicaragua; and for three years, taught yoga at the White House for Michelle Obama's anti-obesity initiative (2011-2013). Peter's influence through his teaching, writing and innovative design has been felt worldwide, and his light-hearted approach with LEVITYoga™ offers unique insight to the evolving art of yoga.

www.LevitYoga.com

The Active Power of Divine Love
by Teri Degler

In the early seventies, I saw a brilliantly colored poster emblazoned with a quote by Tolstoy: "The sole meaning of life is to serve humanity." This saying moved me profoundly, but even in those days – heady, idealistic, and impassioned as they were – I sensed it was, perhaps, a bit over the top. What's more, I later discovered it was not only a very loose translation, it was also taken completely out of context. Still, even all these years later, something about those words rings true with me.

This is not because I believe serving humanity is the *sole* meaning of life, but because I've come to believe it hints at a fundamental truth about the nature of the universe.

I've spent a good deal of my life as a writer researching the lives of the great saints, mystics, and visionaries from the world's various spiritual traditions. When these men and women describe their mystical experiences they almost always talk about a sense of union or a "oneness" with the Divine. It is not just that they say they *saw* the Divine; they make it clear that they have experienced an actual merger with it. In many cases, this is expressed not just as a Union with God – or whatever name they give the divinity – but as a Oneness with all humanity or even all things.

When the 12th century visionary, St. Hildegard of Bingen, wrote about what she called "a reflection of the Living Light" she said her soul – clearly permeated by and at one with this divine light – "rises up high into the vault of heaven and into the changing sky and spreads itself out among different peoples, although they are far away from me in distant lands and places." A couple of centuries later, the Kashmiri saint Lal Ded put it succinctly when she describes reaching *samadhi*: "I diffused the inner light and within, without, all was light."

If this is so – and visionaries from virtually every time and culture have said it was – we have to accept that we really are all One. And, if *this* is so, it makes sense that we need to take care of each other – to serve humanity.

But how does this become meaningful in our lives? The mere intellectual realization of "oneness" doesn't seem to cut it. Once again, the great mystics give us the answer, for when they describe their experiences of Oneness, they usually also talk about love – not just about feeling love, but being flooded and overwhelmed by an awe-filled, indescribable love.

To express this essentially inexpressible experience, the mystics often symbolize it as a passionate union with the Beloved. The 12th c. South Indian saint Mahadevi Akka, for instance, renounces a kingdom to become One with her Beloved, the divine Shiva, who she says has ravaged her heart, taken all of her, and "claimed as tribute" her pleasure. And the renowned Sufi poet Rumi tells us he fell at his Beloved's feet "and no one knew who was the lover and who was the beloved."

But there are times when the great mystics feel separated from the Beloved and long for re-union. Mahadevi Akka cries out that she grieves for her Beloved all day and is mad for him all night. Mechthilde of Magdeburg – a 13ᵗʰ c. Catholic nun and visionary – pleads for an angel to tell her Beloved that his bed is ready and that she is "weak with longing for him".

Like the mystics, we too, are often filled with longing. We might yearn to help end the suffering we see around us, to save Mother Earth, or to know who we truly are – and to express that true, divine self in some creative or other positive way in the world.

But unlike the mystics, we don't realize that this yearning to do good – in whatever way – is a longing for Oneness that is being motivated by divine love. Hildegard pictured this divine love as a cosmic feminine form that she called Caritas. Caritas spoke to Hildegard and motivated her to write, to compose music, to be a healer, and to stand up valiantly for the rights of the wronged.

In Tantric yogic terms this Divine Feminine is called, in her cosmic form, Shakti. In her individualized form – embodied within each one of us – she is known as kundalini-shakti, or just kundalini. The great Kashmiri yogi, Gopi Krishna, wrote extensively on kundalini-shakti as an evolutionary energy that was propelling us along the path to the ultimate goal of yoga: Oneness.

The renowned Jesuit priest, Teilhard de Chardin, called this goal the Omega Point and wrote about an "Eternal Feminine" which was calling to us, urging us, along on this evolutionary journey. Speaking as the Eternal Feminine, he writes, "I am still, as I was at my birth, the summons to unity with the universe."

In this sense, our yearning can be seen as the voice of Shakti. Call her the Eternal Feminine or the active power of Divine Love, it makes no difference. All we have to do to have meaning – deep, enriching, soul-satisfying meaning – in our lives is to listen to Her.

❧✿❧

Teri Degler, award-winning author who has eleven books to her credit, including *The Fiery Muse: Creativity and the Spiritual Quest*. A long-time student of yoga philosophy, mystical experience, and the divine feminine known in yoga as kundalini-shakti. Her freelance writing on topics ranging from environmental activism to parenting have appeared in *Family Circle, More Magazine,*

Today's Parent and many other publications. Her books have been translated into French, German, and Italian, and her latest, *The Divine Feminine Fire: Creativity and Your Yearning to Express Your Self*, became a #1 Amazon Bestseller in Canada in two of spiritual categories.
www.TeriDegler.com

References
Kaul, Jayalal. *Lal Ded*.New Delhi: Sahitya Akademi, 1973, pp. 122-123.
Newman, Barbara. *Sister of Wisdom: St. Hildegard's Theology of the Feminine*. Berkeley: University of California Press, 1987, pp. 6-7.
Ramanujan, A. K., Ed and trans. *Speaking of Shiva*. London: Penguin Books, 1973, p 125.
Tobin, Frank, trans. *Mechthild of Magdeburg: The Flowing Light of the Godhead*. New York: Paulist Press, 1998, p. 43.
Teilhard de Chardin, Pierre. Trans. Hague, René. "The Eternal Feminine" in *Writings in Time of War*. New York: Harper & Row, 1968, p. 197.
Schimmel, Annemarie. *I Am Wind, You Are Fire: The Life and Works of Rumi*. Boston & London: Shambhala, 1992, p. 18.

Meaningful Lives Require Faith and Love
by Raymond Angelo Belliotti

A human life is minimally meaningful if and only if it embodies enough freely chosen interests, projects, purposes, and commitments to engage the bearer and animate his or her faith in life. These interests, projects, purposes and commitments connect a life to value or to other meaning. A minimally worthwhile life is one worth living, a life such that one would not be better off dead or never having been born. The activities that bring minimal meaning must be appropriate to the experience, they must be real not simulated, not induced through external agency, nor merely hallucinations. But the bar of a meaningful life is quite low. Lives are worth continuing and minimally meaningful where great achievement is lacking. Minimal meaning produces enough satisfaction of desires and interests to block suicide or justified voluntary euthanasia.

Minimally meaningful lives typically are connected to lesser or to fewer values and meanings, or more tenuously to value and meaning generally than are robustly meaningful lives.

Some lives are more meaningful than other lives. Robustly meaningful lives, the ones to which we aspire, embody interests, projects, purposes, and commitments that produce significance. A robustly meaningful life is significant, sometimes important, and occasionally even exemplary. We, typically, hope not merely to maintain our lives, but to strive for our vision of a good life. To be significant a life must influence the lives of others in uncommon ways. A significant life leaves historical footprints. To be important a life must be significant enough to make a relatively enduring difference in the world. These historical footprints express, thereby making more public, the importance of the life. To be exemplary, a life must be meaningful, significant, important, and valuable enough to serve as a model or ideal.

Most of us do not have stunningly significant and important lives, although almost all of us do affect the lives of others. Most of our lives fall somewhere between minimally meaningful and robustly meaningful lives. The degree and manner of influence is crucial. To be valuable, lives must be linked to and support value. Some of the more important types of value are moral, cognitive, aesthetic, and religious. A valuable life is always meaningful, but a meaningful life may not be valuable.

If our actions fit into a reasonably coherent scheme, are not futile in that we can in principle achieve our goals or at least make valuable progress toward them, and have purposes within our life scheme, we have no good reason to think our lives are meaningless or that they are absurd. Even if life as a whole lacks inherent meaning, particular lives can range from minimally to robustly meaningful. Some lives, however, fail even to fulfill the criteria of minimal meaningfulness. Such lives are literally not worth living.

The best way to understand meaning in life, is relationally. We gain meaning by connecting to and standing in a relationship with value, significance, and importance. As long as we are limited beings, we can always imagine beings or things of lesser limitations, and bemoan our relative insignificance. We cannot guarantee wise and creative use of the cosmic perspective— that measures human life from the external vantage point of an indifferent cosmic observer. The cosmic perspective is always available to bring us down, if we so choose. But why should we so choose? The metaphor of a telescope suggests that we should use the cosmic perspective and the personal perspective—that evaluates human life from the internal vantage point of a person living his or her life—artfully in order to facilitate meaning and value.

Much of the meaning of life is in the process: imagining and dreaming, planning and organizing, integrating and striving. The metaphor of a pogo stick (or slinky toy) suggests that human beings bound through life in a continuous process that includes purposive goals and related consummations that engender new goals, and so on. The process is valuable in that instead of merely covering the same dreary ground we continuingly self-create. Time spent on matters of more enduring importance such as great music, classical drama, philosophical reflection, and intense personal relationships is often of greater importance than time spent on more mundane matters such as watching television programs with limited shelf time or engaging in meaningless small talk to pass time. This judgment stems from the transcendent nature of the more important matters, how they point to values and meaning beyond themselves. Loving and being loved, pursuit of truth, integrity, courage, the overcoming of obstacles, conscious self-creation, integration with a social network, all define the life of excellence more closely than material accumulation, social approval, and the quest for fame as self-validation.

Meaningful lives require faith and love. We must adopt some form of Nietzsche's *amor fati*. We must love life and the world. We must give the world our fullest response. We must expand our subjectivity through connections and relationships. We will experience our lives as meaningful only if we present the requisite attitude to the world. To do all, or any, of this we must have faith. Reason cannot support our convictions and actions all the way down.

The search for meaning, emboldened by values that point to but never reach the eternal, is too often obscured by our lives of habit and diversion.

We must learn to appreciate life as an endlessly dynamic process of change, not a fixed state. We must understand that a robustly meaningful life, married to a joyous or peaceful psychological condition that is earned, defines high aspirations.

And then we must live.

❧ ❧

Raymond Angelo Belliotti, SUNY Distinguished Teaching Professor of Philosophy, is the author of 18 books including *What is the Meaning of Human Life?* (2001).

Life Has Meaning... Not In Words But In The Living
by Angela Farmer

At the age of three or four years, I knew without a doubt that I came from the sun and that all I had to do was shine!

Each night at bed-time my brother and I knelt by our mother to repeat a simple prayer that included the line, "Please forgive me for my sins".

One day I stopped and said, "I don't think I have any sins", to which my mother quickly replied, "Oh yes you do". I was quite clear in my mind that the day had flowed without a shadow, so I said again, "No there were no sins today". Back came the sentence that blocked out 'my sun' with a big cloud,

"Well you were born in sin".

Now there was no escape and from then on guilt and shame coloured my life. Sometimes I felt guilty for things I never did, ashamed for simply being who I was!

My 'inner sun' never fully left but I had lost the pure shining light. From time to time over the years windows of 'peak awareness' opened and I would catch a glimpse of beautiful light, clarity, overwhelming beauty and deep wisdom. These momentary awakenings, when time stood still and my consciousness expanded gave courage, insights and fresh direction in life, inspired my practice and teaching and brought me together with Victor to this sacred valley of olive trees near the sea on the island of Lesvos Greece.

Here the healing powers of Nature abound and I can slip back inside to a place so ancient and yet familiar ...   far back inside my body like withdrawing into a cave where I feel safe and can receive......

....receive impressions, sounds, information, advice from the invisible beyond me or deep inside and most important of all.....love. I receive the love of the plants, the cold sea, the hot thermal waters, birdsong, animals with their mysterious ways and sometimes people.

In opening to receive, strange as it may seem ...... we are received!

It seems to me that the meaning of life though different for each of us, has much to do with stopping, becoming aware of our breathing and just feeling grateful to life ... the fact that we are alive! From there everything else happens. Our senses open up, our muscles relax, we begin to feel back in to our bodies and although it does not stop the painful things that happen, the pain, the losses, the grief ...those too are part of this experience, those too will pass.

This experience became even more poignant recently with the Refugee arrivals on our shores just a few meters from our home. To have such intimate, heart-rending connections helping people you have never met before, who speak another language, wear different clothes and have risked their children's and their own lives to cross the sea in an over-crowded raft or boat, was a gift and life-changing opportunity. A chance to step back and receive and thus be received by these open and most warm-hearted people. To hug strangers, dry babies, find food and clothes for them realizing they were our family too became the gift.

Life has so much meaning now when I remember to return inside and simply be present. I become then one with my surroundings, a tiny part of this mysterious thing called life and my soul no longer yearns to fill the gaping hole made so long ago.

I receive so much from the trees, the songs of birds, from the waves I swim through and the wild winds of this island that after 75 years, the little child has found again the sun inside and shines!

Of course it is a work in progress and will continue to be so, no doubt until I die but life has enormous meaning now...not in words but in the living.

Although hard to see sometimes in the tragedies that happen around us in the world and in our personal lives, each breath and every time we soften back behind the eyes, behind the heart we expand and are there to hold, to feel, to see, to taste the pain, the joy, the magnificence of it all in this moment.

❧❀❀

Angela Farmer is teaching Yoga courses together with Victor on Lesvos and offering workshops and Womens' retreats around the world.
www.angela-victor.com

The Love of the Eternal One
by Drs. J.J. & Desiree Hurtak

The meaning of life is our quest for Unity within the pluralistic richness of humanity and the discovery of 'Infinite Being'. We are on schoolhouse Earth to discover our inner resources that connect us with the universe of Consciousness and the Infinite Godhead. This inner discovery of the Divine brings us Joy, Love and Wisdom that heals the separation within our Hearts, Minds and Spirits.

It is also the call of our heart that brings higher insights into our mind. Each of us is called to listen and honor our hearts, to nourish ourselves deeply, but few of us know our true higher essence is that of an "Overself" directly connected with the Divine Mind. The awakening to our higher selves reveals the heartbeat of unconditional Service to Life as our foundation of Being, our Truth, in reality, our Divine-Human partnership. As we participate with the Divine Mind, we move into a harmonizing of the world of material form with the heartbeat of Unconditional Love.

Historically, we are made to think of ourselves as individuals, separated from everything around us. This is the illusion of life that blocks us from knowing life's true meaning. To break the illusion of separation, we must also awaken to what

German philosophers and writers call the *"Beruf,"* the Call of the Spirit, to motivate our actions, to become part of a Universal Oneness and to know that we all share in fellowship and Love, activating our greater spiritual Vision.

As important as the power of Love is within Life, it is equally important to join Love with Wisdom to understand our existence as part of a Higher Evolution and the empowerment of knowing we are part of myriad intelligences in a multidimensional, multiverse. With this Wisdom, we can unify scientific evolution and consciousness evolution in the elevation of all Life.

Throughout Life, wherever we look, we can behold its beauty, but as we look within, we discover the spiritual values that exist from our Human-God partnership. When we become open to the movements of the Divine Light, we are fed the energetic sparks that allow us to make a difference in raising consciousness within ourselves and, in turn, help all life on planet Earth. The Meaning of Life is, ultimately, our receiving and sharing of the Love of the Eternal One, which nourishes the quality of our being and the world around us. Our story on Mother Earth is also to unify with the Divine Mother, who created all life, and to find joyous meaning within the Christ body throughout the Cosmos.

Drs. **J.J. Hurtak** and **Desiree Hurtak** are social scientists, spiritual philosophers and authors who have worked in a variety of areas from archaeology and indigenous cultures to planetary science and space law. They are founders of The Academy For Future Science, an international non-profit organization working in association with the United Nations.

Dr. J.J. Hurtak is best known for his writing of *The Book of Knowledge: The Keys of Enoch*® translated into over twenty languages. He is co-author of the *End of Suffering* that he wrote with his colleague, physicist Russell Targ. Together, the Hurtaks have written numerous books including commentaries on the Coptic texts of the *Pistis Sophia* and *The Gospel of Mary*, and their recent books, *Overself Awakening* and *Mind Dynamics*, the latter co-authored with Dr. Elizabeth Rauscher. They have also produced music and won awards for their numerous films that give an in-depth look at science and consciousness development.
www.FutureScience.org

The Moments of Love Between Birth and Death
by Cynthia Brix

The meaning of life is to remember who we are, and to live from the depths of our true being— including who we are in relation to each other and in relation to God (or the Beloved, the Divine Feminine/Masculine, or ultimate reality, whatever name you choose). This is an I-We-Thou reciprocal relationship.

From childhood I have known from the deepest part of myself – at a soul level – that the meaning of life is this reciprocal relationship based in unconditional love, and that the ultimate way to realize this highest love is through selfless service in the world.

We are born from love and we die back into love. The moments in-between create our life journey and the opportunity to learn how to be with love, be in love, *BE* love itself. Through loving, compassionate relationship with ourselves, other humans, and non-humans we begin to discover who we are, and to *realize* that we are not separate from the Beloved – from God.

Of course, in our human condition we stumble, we fall, we make a mess of things, and we get hurt and betrayed, so we have to pick ourselves up again and again in order to love again and again. Our struggles, challenges, and wrestlings throughout life are the grist for the spiritual mill that guides our evolutionary growth. When we open ourselves to the highest love and allow ourselves to be broken by love, we come into a greater place of wholeness and ultimately union with God.

We see this call to love proclaimed throughout many traditions. In the Judeo-Christian tradition, for example, the first commandment is to love God with all your heart, your soul, your mind, your strength. This same teaching is given in the Bhagavad Gita as the supreme secret: to give all your love to the divine, and that we are God's beloved. Similarly in Islam and Sufism; the entirety of Sufism can be summed up in the verse from the *Quran*: "He loves them and they love Him." Love is the foundation of life, and scriptures across the traditions point us to this love. Even those who have no relationship to the spiritual traditions have access to that supreme mystery. When atheists would ask Sri Eknath Easwaran how to practice meditation when they didn't believe in God, he would ask them if they believed in their own higher consciousness. This is the highest aspiration of any of us: when we attune to our highest purpose, it brings meaning to life.

Some of my earliest childhood memories are of watching Martin Luther King, Jr. on the television. I was just three years old when I saw him declare "I have a dream!— that one day . . . little black boys and black girls will be able to join hands with little white boys and white girls, as sisters and brothers." In my little girl heart, this dream took deep root in me as a prayer. I knew that the more people I could become friends with who were different from me, the more I would know God. That prayer bore fruit just a few years later, when I volunteered to be bussed into an all black school, as part of an integration program in my city. That time was some of the best of my childhood.

A few years ago, while facilitating one of our Gender Equity and Reconciliation International trainings in South Africa, I looked around the circle of dark skinned and light skinned people, lesbian, gay, heterosexuals, people of different religions and cultures, and I suddenly realized that I was, in my chosen vocation, living the truth of King's dream. My prayer had become reality—once again.

We all come from the same source, breathe the same air, bleed the same blood, and our hearts beat in continuous rhythm together. Until we are all liberated from the pain and suffering and oppressions of this world, none of us are free. As Cornel West said, "Never forget that justice is what love looks like in public."

For me, the meaning of life is the path of the heart and of service. This is why we are here. In practice this means a commitment to keep working on myself growing toward wholeness, while inwardly remaining in constant remembrance of the Divine, and outwardly engaging in loving, compassionate service in the world.

૨૦ૐ૨૦

Rev. Cynthia Brix, PhD (Hon) is an ordained contemplative interfaith minister and co-director of Satyana Institute. She is co-founder of the Gender Equity and Reconciliation International (GERI) project which conducts training programs for healing and reconciliation between women and men in South Africa, Kenya, Australia, India, UK, Colombia, and North America. Cynthia is co-author of *Women Healing Women*, and contributing author of *Divine Duality: The Power of Reconciliation between Women and Men.*
www.GRworld.org
www.DawnofInterSpirituality.org

Tuning Into the Love Channel
by Bernie S. Siegel

Life of itself has no meaning. It is simply a mechanical event. It presents us with the opportunity and physical ability to be creative and connect with our Lord and the process of creation and create a meaningful life. If we were provided with a perfect world there would be no place for creation or meaning. It would simply be a magic trick. The meaning comes from how we use our minds and bodies and whether we contribute to or become destructive to the process of creation. When we have the opportunity to choose from what is placed before us; life and death, good and evil meaning arises. The meaning our life takes on relates to choosing life and who or what we see as our Lord. Our Lord can be material things and selfish choices based upon our desires and feelings or it can be a chance to love the world, and our neighbors, when we have the right Lord.

Choosing life means we choose life-enhancing behavior for all living things, through our actions and behavior. Then our lives take on meaning. We symbolically represent the same opportunities and elements as a satellite dish, a remote control and a TV screen. A satellite dish has access to many channels and programs and with our remote control we can select which channel we tune into and watch the program displayed.

The problem is there are many Lords out there for us to choose from like all the channels available to you and your remote control. In our case our mind is like the remote and chooses what it tunes into and what it is exposed to and learns from about life and meaning. Then our body, like the TV screen, displays which Lord and programs we have been watching and learning from and thus our life and activities take on meaning.

If our Lord is the Lord of revenge, due to a life experience of indifference, rejection and abuse, and not love then the meaning of our life will be totally destructive as all the headlines reveal. But when you realize we are all here to contribute love to the world, in a way we select, and not one imposed upon us, then our life takes on meaning and becomes joyful experience no matter what profession or lifestyle you choose.

Thus the meaning of life is to give each human being the opportunity to live a genuine and authentic life dedicated and devoted to life enhancing behavior. When we submit to what others impose upon us we lose our life and its meaning. When we abandon our untrue selves and tune into the Lord of love channel every action we take is real, meaningful, lifesaving and life enhancing for all living things of every species residing on this planet we all call home.

So the meaning of life is to give us the opportunity to make our Lord and Creator happy.

❦

Bernie Siegel, M.D. is an internationally recognized expert in the field of cancer treatment and complementary, holistic medicine. In 1978, he originated Exceptional Cancer Patients (ECaP), a specific form of individual and group therapy. His books *Love, Medicine, and Miracles; Peace, Love, and Healing*; and *How to Live between Office Visits* are classics in the field of healing. *Bernie has been named one of the top 20 Spiritually Influential Living People on the Planet by the Watkins Review.*
www.BernieSiegelMD.com

The Meaning Of Life — It All Comes Down to Love

by Meredith Hogan

When I was a newborn baby my mother took me out into the May sunshine and sang to me while she nuzzled the soft lush petals of a pale pink peony into my nose and cheeks. With that single gesture of nurturing motherhood she opened my world. In that moment my life's compass was set and I knew to my core that life is a gift of beauty.

As I grew I (of course) experienced the full spectrum of darkness, depression, pain, longing, illumination and ecstasy. Each experience brought more compassion and stronger desire to know and trust spirit as an ever present indwelling lover and friend. Each contraction becomes an opportunity to grow again. I believe we have come to the planet to expand our consciousness as we dissolve the limitations that keep us small and separate. Embodiment being a powerful key to our energetic healing and liberation from suffering.

In my tradition when we open sacred space we call in the four directions, thank our shared earth mother for all her nourishment and support and then thank the great spirit of life for the gift of one more day to sing and dance the song of creation. To me, that's it. To sing and dance this great song of life together. To be ourselves completely to share our gifts, to serve one another and to hold the world and all it's inhabitants in love as we all move in the direction of our chosen destiny.

❧❧❧

Meredith Hogan is a yogini, singer, dancer and healer. A humble and constant student of life, Meredith was born with an understanding that at the core of human existence, we are all sound and light. She recently released her debut album Saturn Returns with her band GOODBYE GEMINI, a sacred healing record that weaves elements of ancient mantras, modern beats and contemporary electronic based musings.
www.TheShaktiFactory.com

Soaring as a Soul
by Stephanie Marohn

The meaning of life is soul growth and opening our hearts—to the self, to other people, to beings of all kinds, to all of nature, and to the divine. Through all these forms of connection, we grow our souls and move ever closer to fully embodying love and compassion.

By turning inward and clearing all the internal obstacles to an open heart, we clear our way to loving connection with the outer world and the realization that all is one. Understanding that everything in the universe is connected and everything we think and do has an effect brings us to responsibility for our thoughts and actions.

The meaning of life is to soar as a soul, finding the wings of living to our highest potential, sharing the gifts and the heart we were sent here to share with the world.

Loving connection requires that we recognize and honor the sovereignty of others, that is, their right to a full existence. In honoring their sovereignty, we support them in living to their highest potential. This is as true of a river or a mountain as it is of a human and other animals.

Through nourishing our own soul growth and that of others, we advance the consciousness of the planet.

❦

Stephanie Marohn is the author of ten books, including *What the Animals Taught Me: Stories of Love and Healing from a Farm Animal Sanctuary, The Natural Medicine Guide to Autism*, and *The Natural Medicine Guide to Bipolar Disorder*. She runs the Animal Messenger Sanctuary, a safe haven for farm animals, and has an energy healing and animal communication practice for animals.
www.StephanieMarohn.com

Love – From Mortal Mind to Heart
by Altazar Rossiter

Whenever I hear *'What is the Meaning of Life'* question I think of *The Hitch Hiker's Guide to the Galaxy* by Douglas Adams. In his books he asked the meaning of life, the universe and everything. The answer was revealed as 42, and I think that's as good an answer as any in a world where the quest to know everything about everything is a mainstream philosophical objective.

The thing about meaning is that nothing means anything intrinsically of itself. Things, be they abstract or solidly physical, are what they are. When I consider the significance of anything it always involves a context, which *means* the meanings I understand are the meanings I've created myself, and they may have little or no relevance to anyone else.

If I'm not careful, this is where I run into a need to validate my meaning by getting others to agree with me. And if they don't I could get very upset, especially if the meaning they make is somehow in opposition to mine.

When people identify with their meaning that meaning becomes an existential issue. If that meaning is in danger of being demolished intense survival fears can be triggered. These can ultimately degenerate into a rationale for one person to want to eliminate another.

So making meaning can be dangerous, and announcing an opinion on the meaning of life could somewhat ironically be life-threatening. But I'm going to take the risk.

For me, the meaning of my life is to experience being a physical expression of love. This might sound a bit trite, arrogant or naive to some, and this leads me back to the process of making meaning. This is my meaning, I don't insist that you make it yours.

Love is another of those ineffables that defy definition, but I believe most people have experienced it whether they know it or not – a bit like life. It goes unrecognised and submerged in the ocean of emotion and sentimentality that passes itself off as love in the realm of human interaction.

The thing about love is that it's been hijacked by conventions in the mainstream realities we inhabit and it's loaded with the distortions of the mind's attempt to figure it out. When one person says to another "I love you" it's often the beginning of negotiations that lead through a heap of expectations and associated disappointments, and the corresponding landscape of approval – or otherwise.

Conventional concepts of love are riddled with conditions that can be articulated as *I'll be nice to you, if you'll be nice to me.* These conditions all actually mean *I'll pretend not to notice your lack of integrity with yourself, if you'll pretend not to notice mine.*

Life then really becomes a struggle to make sense of what is being felt, as if it wasn't always. But piloting a course through the minefield of emotion emphasises the inadequacy of [what I call] the *mortal mind* to cope with feelings. And this scares the mortal mind, because it wants to control everything, but it has no authority over feelings. What it is able to do is trigger emotions – or more accurately emotional reactions.

The mortal mind is very good at triggering emotional reactions, which are nothing less than a smokescreen that prevent the experiential truth of living from being felt. I see this as a fundamental disconnection from the flow of personal well-being that is endemic in the world today. The existential psychosis of fear and control that underwrite mortal mind-sets and false beliefs is obscured in the confusion that ensues.

Love is marginalised. The domination of mortal mind-sets, in what is hubristically called the civilised world, successfully overlaps cultural imperatives in the collective to create a blanket of doctrine, dogma and ideology that's basically woven from a fear that isn't real.

My personal history has been to learn that my mortal mind is *not* me, even though it thinks it is. By default, this has involved trusting what I feel in my heart over what my mortal mind wants to believe, and deconstructing the emotional reactions that are triggered when it fears for its existence.

I'm a work in progress. I don't pretend for one moment that I experience myself as love all the time, or even most of the time. But I do some of the time. And when I do it's very clear that my life has meaning.

❧✿❧

Altazar Rossiter PhD is an holistic mentor, energy facilitator and wisdom teacher. He leads a modern mystery school programme based in the Netherlands. This embraces the new energy paradigm of self-empowerment that's arising in human consciousness, in a co-creative partnership with Spiritual Intelligence.

Altazar is the author of *Developing Spiritual Intelligence – The Power of You*, and facilitates the deeply transformative process of partnering with Spiritual Intelligence in public workshops. He lives quietly in the UK with his partner of over 20 years. www.AltazarRossiter.com

Realizing the Field of Love
by Sarah McLean

Does anyone really know the answer to the question, *"What is the meaning of life?"*

I am going to imagine you are asking. You, yes you, the one reading these words.

The purpose of life is to become utterly aware of the source of your life, of all lives, and in fact, of all of creation. I believe the source of your life is love. It is the same love that moves the mountains, that moves you, and that it is inherent in everything. Some people would call this love God, others, the creative field of intelligence, some, the field of love, or your true nature. It doesn't matter what you call it. What matters is that you have the direct experience of it and come to realize this love is inside you and all around you.

For a moment, turn your attention to that which is looking through your eyes, and reading these words. What is there? What is that? Now listen to the sounds in the room you are in. Who is it who is listening, what is this "you" that is attending to and aware of these sounds?

As you just experienced, you have the power to focus your attention where and how you want. And, we know from physics, that there is an observer effect. Your gentle, natural attention has an effect on the world around you.

Once you begin to become aware of your attention, you inevitably will become more intimate with its source.

Consider the question again, who is it who was reading, and listening? Consider from what/where this attention arises.

Your attention arises from your awareness — a field of love and light. You can think of your attention as a currency. And a valuable one. It is the currency of love, and you can use it like a flashlight, shining its beam onto what you wanted illuminate.

What happens to that which you truly give your natural attention to, whether it's your body, your plants, your education, your environment, your pets, your partner, or your kids? I imagine your attention nourishes the relationship. What does it feel like to be paid kind attention? Does it feel like love? Perhaps your attention is love. Knowing this, you just might start to become more in charge of to what and to whom you "pay" your attention.

You can't think your way to this realization. In fact, the more you think about what I am writing about, the less you will realize it.

The way I, and many people before me, have been able to awaken to this reality is through meditation.

Meditation, when practiced correctly, without preconceived ideas, allows you to become intimate with your interior. Meditation is a practice that settles the fluctuations of the mind—thought is transcended. With mediation you then can have the direct experience of the source of your awareness. And this realization changes everything.

I hope you too realize the source of your life—the field of love—the creative intelligence that infuses all that is. You will always find what you are looking for, and you will come to realize that what you are seeking is in fact seeking you. My prayer for everyone is this: may you awaken to the love that lives through you as you. May you realize your true nature.

❧⁂☙

Sarah McLean is a global go-to teacher for contemporary meditation and mindfulness who has been teaching mediation for over 20 years. Sarah founded the McLean Meditation Institute in Sedona, Arizona in 2006, a community meditation center which offers drop in meditations and classes in meditation and mindfulness practices. Sarah is the author of *Soul-Centered: Transform Your Life in 8 Weeks with Meditation* and *Love & the Power of Attention.*
www.McLeanMeditation.com

Our Beloved Essence
by Yogi Dada Gunamuktananda

What is the meaning of life?

I don't know the answer to that question. Which really means I know the answer to that question. Because, as the saying goes, *"He who thinks he knows, does not know. He who knows he does not know, knows."*

What?

I know!

But here's an answer based on the teachings of my guru, someone infinitely wiser and more capable of answering this question than me. It's also based on the experience I've gained from my meditation practice over the last 25 years.

The purpose of our lives is to realize ourselves. In the yogic tradition this is called "self-realization." We all have a sense of self; of self associated with our body, our mind, and our relationship between our body, mind and the people and things of the world: our family, friends, possessions, surroundings, our community, society and the wider world.

But we also have a deeper sense of self, our spirit, the essence of which is the love and peace, the infinite happiness or bliss, that we all yearn for. No matter who we are, no matter where we come from, no matter what our race, culture or religion may be, we all want the same thing. We may call it love, we may call it peace, we may call it happiness. But whatever we call it we all know what it is. It's that deepest feeling of being and connectedness within us all. It's our most precious feeling of self at the core of our existence. It's our beloved essence.

Now, according to yogic philosophy, our own sense of self is part of a greater self. In fact, our own self is not only part of, but one with, the greater self. Our own consciousness is one with the infinite consciousness of the universe, just as the waves on the surface of the sea are one with the sea. The more we realize our own consciousness as the one infinite universal consciousness, the more we satiate our innermost longing for bliss, because bliss, or infinite happiness, is the essence of infinite consciousness.

So in order to attain what we ultimately want deep within ourselves we must look within ourselves. This process is called meditation. Meditation is not about anybody telling you what you should believe or experience. Meditation is the process of looking within yourself, of strengthening the connection to your deepest sense of self, of finding the essence of yourself within yourself and realizing that essence as the essence of the greater self that pervades all people and all things, the universal self.

This is inevitable for each and every one of us. It's our destiny to realize ourselves as the one infinite and universal self. That's why we have a thirst for limitlessness, for perfect peace and contentment, infinite happiness or bliss, because the bliss we are all searching for is the essence of ourselves. There's a beautiful paradox here. Our inner self and our final destiny are one and the same. We don't actually have to become anything other than what we already are. We only have to realize ourselves. We are all on a journey towards realizing ourselves in the deepest possible sense; as the essence of our own existence and of all existence. We are all on a journey that will ultimately culminate in the total and permanent realization of infinite bliss for each and every one of us.

That realization will not only be the consummation of our deepest life's desire, but the more we realize our own existence as the essence of the universal existence, the universal consciousness, the more we will also feel the essence of everyone else as our own essence too; that everyone is part of us just as all waves are part of the same sea. Our own existence is one with the existence of all others. In fact, at the deepest level there are no others. We are all one. Another beautiful paradox. And it is that realization which will facilitate the greatest peace, contentment and bliss within us all and amongst us all, because the more we realize our oneness with others — all people, animals, plants, our planet, the entire universe — the more love we will feel for others too, because we will feel others as one with ourselves. The more we feel our own self as one with the cosmic self, the more we feel all others as one with our own self. And the more we love others as one with our own self, and feel the destiny of others as one with our own destiny, the more empathetic we will be, the more loving we will be, the more compassionate, the better our relationships, and the more willing and able we will be to help others and to make this world a better place.

So the purpose of our lives is self-realization. And translating that realization — that expanded feeling of self — into loving others; including all within the embrace of our love; helping all to attain their inner destiny; our one collective destiny. There's another beautiful paradox here. At the heart of our own emancipation lies the emancipation of us all.

୧🐚ᴥ୧🐚

Yogi Dada Gunamuktananda, meditation teacher of Ananda Marga, where one can sign up to a free online meditation course.
www.AnandaMarga.org

Remembering the Divine Source
by Jacqui Lalita

When all your desires are distilled;
You will cast just two votes: to love more, and be happy.
~Hafiz

Here we all are on this lush rock of a planet spiraling through space! What are the odds? Why have we come so far and endured so much to be here?

I believe the answer is quite simple. In essence, we've come here to love, to be happy and in peace, and to help others in kind. What more could we do with the days we are given here than to truly be here now, living in wonder and appreciation, contributing in some way to the collective tapestry being woven together by every sentient creature we share this spiraling world with. To serve and remember the Divine Source from which we've come is a chance we are given each day as we rise. We, who as Rilke says, have been "sent out beyond our recall" have come all this way to recall that very Divine Source of our existence.

We all come with our own unique soul mission, so perhaps the pertinent question is "What is the meaning of *my* life?"

To find our particular soul calling and bring it forth, giving the fullness of the gifts we've been given, this is the work of every soul and will mean something different to each of us. What I've learned in these humble years dancing and singing my praises on this green Earth, is that to surrender myself to my soul's calling is to know the very meaning in my existence.

There is a heat and fire to living, a mystery and unending wonder that reveals itself through the tender throbbing of our wild hearts. This vast ocean of life is beckoning us to plunge into its resplendent waters, that we may be awed into the present moment by the drenching beauty of it all. Come now to the ocean of your days. Dive in and enter life which yearns to live itself through you. Be happy. Be free. Be who you came to be.

May we make it a good one, a good life with right relations and right livelihood. May we uplift all those we come in contact with, shining as sparks of the exquisite flame, living, breathing, speaking, and expressing as radiant emanations of Creation itself.

❧⚘⚘❧

Jacqui Lalita is a mythical storyteller who travels the world teaching traditional dances of the Middle East and devotional dance as a path of healing. She leads rejuvenating retreats for women and is passionate about reawakening the feminine mysteries and igniting divine joy. She is the author of two books of poetry, *Romancing the Divine* and *Rebirth of Venus*. The moon, stars, plants and furry creatures continue to be her greatest teachers. www.DanceOfTheDivine.org

Love Is a Gift
by Marcus Braybrooke

'It is Love that moves the Sun and Stars,' wrote Dante – perhaps Europe's most famous poet – at the end of his long journey through Hell, Purgatory and Heaven. Looking back at my life's journey I too would say that 'Love' is the meaning of life and as I have travelled I have discovered new and ever-deepening dimensions of that Love.

I first experienced love long before I heard the word – I hope at my conception: certainly in the care and love my parents showed me and in the widening circle of the family and first friends. Going to Church, I learned about God's love in Jesus – but also from the beauty and wonder of the countryside I sensed what Wordsworth called 'a presence that disturbs with joy of elevated thoughts.' It was in my early teens that I first sensed God's love in a personal way. I had gone by myself to a swimming pool and over-confidently ventured into the deep end, where I started to drown and only just clambered out in time. Cycling home, words from a prayer kept coming into my mind – 'may we show forth our thanks not all with our lips but by giving up ourselves to your service' – words which I head as a call to be a vicar.

I soon discovered that knowing I was loved by God did not make life any easier at school and certainly not as a conscript in the army – but again I was given words from St Paul to keep my head above water, 'In whatsoever state I am, therewith I am content.'

But I still thought God – rather like a parent – expected me always to be on my best behaviour. I probably went to church too much, but at one service I was overwhelmed by the sense that God loves me just as I am. I realised that God's love is a gift that set me free: but it was the generous love of my dear Mary and the of the family that has made that love a reality.

Love is a gift, but like a plant I had to allow it to grow.

In the heat of South India, where I spent a year after university, it grew quite rapidly. Meeting people of other faiths, visiting temples and mosques, reading some of the Upanishads and the poems of the Tamil saints, I came to see that God's love is for all people and that I could learn from the experience of holy people who had followed a different path. At the time, this was frowned on by Church Leaders.

It was in India too when I was helping at a Leprosy Clinic with some other students one a Muslim, one a Hindu – that I had the dream that people of all faiths were called to serve the poor and to work for peace. Much of my interfaith work has been an attempt to help make that dream a reality.

The greatest challenge to this hope was when I worked for the Council of Christians and Jews and had daily reminders of the horror of the Holocaust both from my reading and from meeting people whose families had been murdered. How can one speak of God's love in the presence of burning children? My picture of God changed. One Rabbi who became a close friend had spent his teenage years in Auschwitz – but it was there that he had had an experience of God. 'The question', he said, 'was not where was God but where was humanity?'

I came to see that God does not exercise his power by over-ruling human behavior, because Love is never coercive. Rather God speaks to us in the cry of the hungry and of the tortured is the cry of God. God puts the future into our human hands.

Looking into the evil also forced me to look within. How would I have behaved in other circumstances? The terrorists also are human beings. I deplore their actions. Yet to respond to hatred with hatred, only adds fuel to the fire. Costly as it is, healing comes from the courage and love to forgive or to weep at what we have done.

Increasingly too, I realise that if we are co-Creators with God, our concern must be for all living beings with whom we share this planet and for the natural world.

'Love is God's meaning,' said Mother Julian of Norwich many centuries ago. Little by little we learn more of its meaning and I hope, as she did, that we shall discover that in this love 'our life is everlasting.'

***

Rev. Dr. Marcus Braybrooke, an Anglican parish priest and interfaith activist, is Joint President of the World Congress of Faiths and Co-Founder of the Faith & Belief Forum. He and his wife Mary, a social worker and magistrate, have participated in many international movements that seek to bring people of all faiths together to work for peace and to help those in need.

Marcus' books – also e-books – include ones on the Bible; introductions for Christians to world religions, books on interfaith and spirituality, including *Beacons of Light – 100 People who have shaped the Spiritual History of Human Kind; Peace in Our Hearts, Peace in Our World*; and edited *1,000 World Prayers and Bridge of Stars*.
www.MarcusBraybrooke.com

Love Alone is the Greatest Power
by Zinovia Dushkova

Many years ago, standing on stage at one of my meetings with readers, I was looking into the audience, inwardly waiting for the moment when the question "What is the meaning of life?" would finally be asked. Yet, to my regret, among the many questions posed, it never came up. At that time, a woman who happened to be visiting me at the time had collected all the notes addressed to me in the auditorium and passed them up to the stage. When we returned home, she laid a couple of these notes on the table, one of which read: "What is the meaning of life?"

"How could one ask such a stupid question?" she said.

But I answered that I had felt this question and, moreover, had actually been waiting for it, as I wished to voice to the whole audience the answer which had always lived in my heart (and still does): "For me, the meaning of life consists in Love!"

And finally, now after almost two decades, thanks to the question asked by Mr. Nicolae Tanase, founder of the "Meaning of Life" e-publication, I can answer this question for a wider audience of readers.

My story of becoming an author began on 27 October 1992. On that day, I wrote the *"Parable of a Heavenly Warrior"*, the essence of which was that he wanted to save the people he loved so much. But this love was not returned by those who were engaged in reckless debauchery. The Warrior piously believed in Divine Love, but evil proved to be too insidious, and so at the hour of battle no one from among the people stretched out their hand, and he was devoured by a black abyss. Faith in Love — this alone helped in destroying the obstacles of gloom and in elevating the Warrior to the heavenly azure, from where he looked at the Earth with the one thought: "To come and triumph by Love."

Since then, this thought has become my motto, as well as the goal of my path. And Love is so multifaceted and so all-embracing in its essence that indeed, any true believer, regardless of their particular religious or denominational adherence, can know this! Only a great heart is able to accommodate all of the Greatest Images of the Teachers of Humanity.

One time, during a train trip through India, a number of madrasa graduates sat next to me, and we talked for several hours about Muhammad, Fatima, and Islam in general. I cited the assertions of Fatima in response to the questions: "Do you love Jesus Christ?" She answered, "Who does not love Him?!" and to "Do you hate Satan?" — "There is so much love in my heart that there is simply no room for hate!"

The next morning, one of the madrasa graduates, upon seeing me without a kerchief on my head, asked me with astonishment: "But aren't you a Muslim?" I replied that I am a Christian. When he wondered how I knew so much about Muslim Saints, I noted that disrespect for other religions was a great sin for a Christian. I said that while a small wrinkled heart was incapable of accommodating even a single image, a heart that is growing and expanding is able to accommodate the images of all: Buddha, Krishna, Muhammad, and others. Later I challenged him: "Would you be able to kill me over the fact that Jesus Christ occupies a greater place in my heart than others?" The Muslim drew aside and said loudly and categorically: "No!"

I told him that I actually experienced feelings of shame because not all Sons of Heaven had yet occupied equal places in my heart, that I still loved some of them more than others... And then I sensed confusion and some kind of internal shock in the soul of the Muslim. Looking into his eyes, I realized that he would make an excellent priest, and in his heart there would certainly be a place for those who bring peace and love into our suffering world...

I will never stop believing that one day people of different religions will be able to see each other as brothers and sisters, and they will not only speak about Saints with admiration, but also imitate their lives, regardless of religious labels.

Many of the Great Saints have experienced the bitterness of persecution and betrayal, the craftiness of tortures, and the gaping lack of love on the part of those to whom they have brought nothing but Love. And so, by following in the footsteps of the Sons of Heaven, we, too, are destined to experience many sufferings ourselves. Yet we are also destined to continue bearing our cross in Joy, for in it alone is Wisdom to be found.

Yes, Love alone is the Greatest Power existing in the Universe. And now, after decades of treading a thorny path, I can repeat only one thing: "The meaning of life consists in Love!"

❧

Zinovia Dushkova, Ph.D., is an award-winning Russian author, poet, philosopher, historian, and traveler who has devoted more than 25 years to the acquisition of the secret wisdom underlying all known religions and philosophies. She has written approximately sixty books of spiritual and ethical content, published in Russia, Ukraine, Moldova, and France. These works are all of a spiritual nature, having been recorded during her travels in the Himalayas, the Karakorum, the Nilgiri, the Gobi Desert, the Pyrenees, and beyond.

Dr. Dushkova continues the spiritual tradition of the hidden Himalayan Masters who guided Helena Blavatsky and Helena Roerich to lead humanity from intellectual knowledge to the divine wisdom of the heart. Thus, in 1995, she gained admittance to the secret *Book of Dzyan* and revealed its new excerpt in *The Book of Secret Wisdom* (Radiant Books, 2015). The experience of communication with one Himalayan Master of Wisdom inspired her to write *Parables from Shambhala* (Radiant Books, 2016). Dr. Dushkova's major work is *The Teaching of the Heart* series (Radiant Books, 2016–2018), which was created during 1997–1998 in the spiritual cooperation with Master Morya — the same Master who was behind the creation of Helena Blavatsky's *The Secret Doctrine* and Helena Roerich's *Agni Yoga*.
www.dushkova.com/en

Love in the Purist Form
by J. Ivy

What is the meaning of life?

Immediately when I hear this question lifelong thoughts fire off. I find myself soul searching, thinking of those moments when I discovered myself, my purpose, my mission and those later moments in life when discovery occurred all over again and again and again...

This question reminds me of so many benchmark moments. The earliest memory being when I was eight or nine in a weekly bible study class ran by my Uncle Granville on the South-Side of Chicago. Sitting there in the store front church along with a circle of adults, he posed a similar question, and without pause, the reflexes of my mind quickly fired off, "Life is a test." Not being hammered by the challenges and heartache life tends to throw at you as you get older I found my young truth to be the right answer resting in my heart. Grown heads nodded in agreement, looks of approval were thrown at me, a few hands clapped, someone patted me on my back, my mother looked at me with so much pride in her eyes. Proud and excited, the thought repeated in my mind. Life is a test...

But now, in my adult years, after having gone through eons of experiences and pertinent life lessons, this question finds me once again...what is the meaning of life? What is the meaning of this "test?"

As I've allowed my gift of poetry to guide me, my spirit has moved me to speak on forgiveness, on self worth, on lifting up the next, on inspiring others, on building your confidence, on using your own gifts, on making a mark, making change, making history and the common denominator for all these elements, for each phase of the "test," has been anchored in rediscovering our purist form of unconditional love. Love for self and love for others. Selfless love...

Love without judgement. Love with no strings or ego or envy attached. Love for blessings. Love for the little things. Love for nature. Love for the institution of family and the friends that become a part of it. Love for the experience for this magical journey we call life. The meaning of life is finding love during the course of these series of test. After all, love is what protects us, it's what leads us to our purpose, it's what charges our spirits and feeds our souls. In my humble opinion and strong belief, finding LOVE in the purist form is the truest meaning of life...

≈❧≈❧

J. Ivy, a NAACP Image Award Winning Poet has been featured on Grammy Award Winning

Platinum Albums with Kanye West, Jay-Z & John Legend. He is the author of two books, *Here I AM: Then & Now* and *Dear Father: Breaking The Cycle of Pain*. J. Ivy's new goal to get one million people to write a letter to their fathers is themed as "One Million Letters Written, One Million Hearts Healed!" As a performance poet and author, Ivy's passionate delivery always leaves spectators transfixed in a state of inspiration. His motto, "Dreams Don't Come True, They Are True" has guided him from his hometown Chicago to hundreds of cities
www.J-Ivy.com

Pouring Love: A Reflection on the Meaning of Life

by Camille Hamilton Adams Helminski

Day by day
we venture
closer;
we turn
the handle
of the door
and enter.
Room upon room
opens
in the vastness
of Your Palace
reaching the heavens
and pouring
water to the earth
through fountains
hovering
mid-air.
Hu[1] would have thought
we could exist,
without
technology,
but only, by heart,
remembering
why we were born!
You treasure
us;

we have been
known,
by Your Love. [2]
Nothing less
dances
through these eyes,
Ya Nur,
Ya Rahim,
Ya Quddus
'alameen,
Ya Hayy,
Ya Qayyum,
Ya Wadud! [3]

1   *Hu* is the pronoun indicating the Divine Presence.
2   "I was a Hidden Treasure and I so loved to be known that
     I created the two worlds, seen and Unseen, in order that
     My Treasure of Generosity and Loving Kindness might be
     known." (Hadith Qudsi, a saying of God conveyed by the
     Prophet Muhammad, peace and blessings be upon him,
     in addition to the Holy Quran)
3   O You Who Are Light, O Infinitely Merciful One, O Most
     Holy and Pure of all Worlds, O Ever-living One, O Eternal
     Self-Subsisting Source of All Being, O Love!

Shaikha Camille Hamilton Adams Helminski has
been a student of the Quran and the traditions of
the Prophets for more than 40 years. Her latest
book, *Ninety-Nine Names of the Beloved*, is a
collection of poetic reflections on the Divine Names

intrinsic to Islam and the Quranic revelation, to support the increased opening of our awareness to all the Generosity and Loving-kindness of the Divine Bestowal.

Camille has also produced some of the first modern English translations of Jalaluddin Rumi, rendered a significant portion of the Qur'an into English in The Light of Dawn, Daily Readings from the Holy Qur'an, and compiled the wisdom of female Muslim saints in the now classic guide, Women of Sufism. Camille and her husband, Kabir, teach internationally through the Threshold Society which they founded in 1988, encouraging all to awaken to the Divine Presence in every moment of our lives.
www.sufism.org

Pure Unlimited Love
by Stephen G. Post

What is the meaning of life?

One thing is for certain – human beings need meaning or they perish. Sometimes, in desperation, they seek meaning in all the wrong places and may even wish to inflict their meaning on others, as seems to be the case with adolescent converts from emptiness to ISIS. The need for meaning is so deep, and the meaninglessness of modern possessive materialism is so great, that it is easy to understand the appeal of things that promise even a brutal new world.

Let us acknowledge that meaning does not come from yet another $200 pair of shoes, and that our modern industrialized countries are clearly rated as less happy than simpler lands with deeper community and sources of spirituality. So we have the terrible waste of lives in addictions, possessive greed, unlimited hedonism, bullying, hatred, consumerism, and even violent extremism.

Let us hope that we also are seeing the dawn of a new more spiritual age of deeper meanings, where we flourish in the surprising fact that in the giving of self lies the discovery of a deeper self. It all comes down to the right kind of love: when the happiness, security and well-being of another is meaningful to me in the sense of being as real as my own happiness, security and well-being, I love that person. We can extend this beyond the nearest and dearest to the neediest as a matter of personal calling, and even to all humanity and nature. For some more mystical people, this love is felt as an underlying energy that sustains the universe and all things both seen and unseen (aka Brahmin, Ultimate Reality, Divine Mind, Supreme Consciousness, "God", etc.). But whether we are secular of religious, spiritually attuned or less so, the bottom line is that the greatest leap forward in human consciousness will come with a deep awareness of pure unlimited love.

It seems that in this age, our need and even our rage for meaning is a tale of two cities, one of unfathomable creative love and the other of equally unfathomable hate. The human future is in doubt, but may we strive to build that first city. In the end, it is best to study and develop here on earth what means most in eternity — love.

❧ ⁖ ☙

Stephen G. Post, PhD., is a best-selling author, leading expert on happiness, health, success and medical school professor. He is President of the Institute for Research on Unlimited Love and Director and Founder of the Center for Medical Humanities, Compassionate Care—Stony Brook University. — www.StephenGPost.com

Life Itself is the Search for Meaning
by Robert Beer

I have come to believe that death alone reveals the true moral and ethical stature of life, and while that life is being lived this issue always hangs in the balance. We are born with amnesia, and develop without recognising our true innate nature, or the dimensions from which we manifest as eternal beings evolving towards self-perfection. So there is no longer the need to incarnate again with amnesia.

The evidence for the continuity of existence beyond death is overwhelming, if one seriously undertakes to explore the various avenues of research into 'Non-local Consciousness' being revealed in our time. This includes all aspects of parapsychology, quantum mechanics, the evidence derived from universal reincarnation studies, after-death communication, deathbed visions, and near-death experiences. The latter relating to the deep 'life-review' component alluded to in my opening sentence. This is experienced as a reliving of one's entire life outside of time, where the consequences of every thought, word and action between one's self and others are vividly and indelibly revealed.

Often an angelic 'being of light' bears witness to this holographic life-review, an all-knowing and absolute embodiment of unconditional love who remains completely non-judgemental. Likewise, the experiential content of one's life-review does not change over time, it remains ever-present and is often described as the 'most real' event that happened in a person's life. Unconditional love is boundless, unchanging, and the after-effects of experiencing such a profoundly unconditional love are always extremely transformational.

Life's Golden Rule of 'doing unto others as you would have them do unto you' never changes, but we can always change. The pure essence of unconditional love is the foundation of all spiritual and religious traditions, and in our present time one does not have to die to know their outcome or validity. We can learn from the accounts of those who have been 'brought back from death' and draw our own conclusions. The sheer consistency of these contemporary afterlife accounts appears to herald a new spiritual paradigm shift in our present time.

Plato's 'Republic' records the earliest NDE in the 'Myth of Er', and Socrates' statement that, a life lived without philosophy – an unexamined life – was not worth living. Philosophy, as the 'love of wisdom', with its three branches; natural (physics), moral (ethics), and metaphysics (what is beyond physics), is eternally fresh and pregnant with meaning, and to believe that life has no meaning points towards an unexamined life.

So what is the meaning of life? Life itself is the search for meaning, for the cultivation of love, wisdom, compassion, sympathetic joy, equanimity, but not necessarily happiness or pleasure, which are often just intervals between two pains.

Way back in the 1970's I can across some graffiti on a London railway bridge, which read: "Death can be god-orgasm if you spend your life in divine foreplay." I can live with this.

"When at last, in a single flash, you attain to full realization, you will only be realizing the Buddha-nature that has been with you all the time; and by all the foregoing stages you will have added nothing to it at all. You will come to look on those eons of work and achievement as no better than unreal actions performed in a dream. Your true nature is something never lost to you in moments of delusion, nor is it gained at the moment of enlightenment."

(Huang Po, 9th century)

❦❦❦

Robert Beer first first began to study and practice Tibetan thangka painting in India and Nepal between 1970-76, and was one of the first westerners to become actively involved in this field. Since then he has devoted most of his life to studying the iconography and symbolism of Indo-Tibetan Vajrayana Buddhist deities. Over the past twenty years he has been actively involved with some of the finest contemporary Newar artists of the Kathmandu Valley, and has assembled a unique collection of their work.

Apart from his continuing work with Indo-Tibetan iconography, he is also deeply involved in researching all aspects of the afterlife, especially the enhanced consciousness and enduring transformative effects of the near-death experience. His illustrations have been published and widely 'pirated' in hundreds of books and websites, and he is the author and illustrator of *The Encyclopedia of Tibetan Symbols and Motifs*, and *The Handbook of Tibetan Buddhist Symbols*.
www.TibetanArt.com

Robert Adams: On Love

Q: Robert, what is love?

Robert Adams: Love, happiness, peace, joy, are all your real nature. It is a feeling beyond the feeling. It is a total ineffable something that you are. It makes you know that you are one with everything. Everyone is your brother and sister. Including the flowers, the trees, the animals, the bedbugs, the cockroaches, the mountains, the sky, the sick people, the healthy people, the poor people, the rich people. When you can look at everyone with one I and not differentiate. Then you're in love.

But when you pick out somebody special and you think that one you're totally in love with because he or she has the right features, the right figure, the right assets that you want, this is infatuation. This only lasts for a day until you get what you want. But true love never changes. It doesn't go away because it never came from anywhere. It's just something that is and you are that.

Q: Please explain specific differences between love and attachment. Thank you.

Robert Adams: Attachment is something you hold onto for your own sake. Because you believe if you don't have the thing you're attached to you'll have problems. You can't live without a certain person, a certain thing. Therefore you're totally attached to a person, place or thing yet in your sick mind you call this love. You think this is love.

Love is absolute freedom without any attachment whatsoever. Love gives, it never takes. Love is letting everything alone, not judging anybody or anything. Allowing it to unfold in its own inimitable way, this is love.

Attachment is when you're thinking of your ego. So you make all kinds of rules and regulations in your life with people, how they must behave to you with objects, things. How they must be possessed by you and you call this love. In other words you love somebody or something because he or she or the something is doing whatever you want them to do. It's pleasing you the way you want to be pleased. So you love that person or place or thing. It's giving you happiness.

For instance when you buy a new car. You love that car with all your heart. You show everybody your car. You talk about your car how beautiful it drives, nice seats, the wooden panel you've got inside. But as soon as the car crashes you've changed your mind.

You have a broken car now, the car has been mashed, to pieces. Therefore you no longer love the car the same way as you did before. As a matter of fact you're thinking of trading in the car for a new one. For the car has become old. It's no longer beautiful as it was.

You do the same with people. When we love someone we say that we love them terribly when we first meet them. Then as time passes and we get older we wish to trade them in for a new model. This was never love, it was attachment. Therefore love is letting go and loving for its own sake. Attachment is never letting go and loving because it satisfies you, gives you something. If the something stops the love stops. That's the difference.

...

What is the meaning of life? Who am I? You are the very answer to these questions. Make your life very simple. Do not be too profound. Do not go looking to teachers and thinking they have a special answer for you. There is no special answer, there is no special teachings. Everything you're looking for is within yourself. Where else would it be? What you are today is a result of all your thinking, throughout the years, through many lifetimes. Your belief system has created the body that you need right now for your next step in evolution. This is why I always say, "You are in your right place. There are no mistakes. You are exactly where you're supposed to be." If you don't like where you are, look within yourself.

No-one can really give you anything for you are the power. There is no power apart from you. Be happy always. Feel the freedom. Feel the bliss. Inquire who you are. The answer will come by itself. Inquire, "What am I doing here? Where did I come from? What am I?" Do not be disturbed by events in this world. Do not take life so seriously. Be of service to humanity. When you see people suffering, help. Come to the aid of the homeless, the poor, the sick. When you realize there is only one who are you helping but yourself. To whom are you giving service but yourself, who is benefitting but yourself.

Be kind, be loving, everything else will take of itself. You are the one, the holy one, the mighty one, the true one, the loving one. Go within your heart right now. Dive deep within the heart centre and lose yourself entirely.

The spiritual heart centre is on the right side of the chest. See a sphere of golden light in the heart center, a sphere of beautiful golden light, throbbing. See this globe of white light, golden light expanding, expanding throughout the whole universe. Where all of the planets, galaxies, everything are superimpositions on this golden globe of light. Everything is an image on this light. Like the image on the screen. This light is like boundless space. It accommodates the whole universe. Everything is in this light. Nothing is left out.

Understand that you are the light. The light is you, the Self. The imperishable Brahman. The ultimate reality, nirvana. The I-am that I-am, that is the nature of this golden light. See all the images disappearing and only the light remains. Feel this light as yourself. You are filled with joy, filled with bliss, with happiness. You are now the true Self and there are no others. Feel this deeply. Feel this bliss, this love, this joy, pulsating within, without you. All of your past has been wiped out. There never was any room for a past or a present or a future. There is just the one mighty Self, expressing itself as consciousness and you are that!

Excerpts from *Robert Adams: Collected Works*

❧❧❧

Robert Adams was an American Advaita teacher.

Universal Love and Compassion
by Nawang Khechog

We must try to live a life with these two principles. First, we try our best not to hurt or harm anyone and then try our best to help and serve anyone within our reach.

Since our human life is much complex and complicated, so we must try to have better education and good enough living facilities and greater inter-connection in life and in the world. So on these foundations we can take care of our own wellbeing as well as we can serve others much greater way. Of course we must try our best not to engage in any harmful actions physically, verbally and mentally. Yes, this must be the basis of our living standard.

Now I am supposed to be an universal Buddhist follower. So I will also try to share some points from this perspective. One of the ancient legends about Tibet says: whoever goes to Tibet, they somehow feel so happy and peaceful. I used to think. Why so?

Yes, it may be because of the pure and beautiful landscape and environment. But I feel it is mainly because it is Mahayana Buddhist culture and practice. For more then a thousand years Mahayana Buddhist teachings captured the imagination of Tibetan Emperors and Tibetan people that all sentient beings are the same as who want happiness and do not want suffering. Therefore, we all must try to practice universal compassion and universal love. Which means we must try not to hurt any sentient beings and try to love them all dearly with whole heart.

The culture is so wide spread that even on the lips of those butchers, would say, Om Mani Padme Hoong, I pray this for all mother sentient beings. This mantra is carved on the rocks and printed on prayer flags, everywhere on the mountains and in every villages and towns. Even a small kid to elderly Tibetan, everyone chants this universal compassion mantra. Almost you can never escape from this atmosphere. In America you can't almost escape from the advertisement of McDonald's and Coca-Cola. In the same way you can not escape from the mantra of universal compassion in Tibet.

The heart of Mahayana Buddhist tradition is such that every sincere practitioner must try to cultivate Universal Compassion and Universal Love, Universal Responsibility and Bodhicitta. Bodhicitta is the supreme heart that one wants to attain Buddhahood (the Highest Enlightenment). So that one can lead all sentient beings to the great freedom from all sufferings and to the supreme happiness, joy and serenity of Buddhahood. Buddha is not a reserved state. We all have Buddha nature and we all can become Buddha. It is like any one born in USA, he or she can become the President of this nation.

His Holiness the Dalai Lama is a great example of a being who can spread the inspiration and atmosphere of such universal love and universal compassion. More than the last one thousand years Tibet has manifested countless such beings and you can imagine what that would do to whole of the nation. Bodhicitta, the universal love and compassion radiates from the heart of all these great beings.

This is my highest meaning of life. Although I am at the very basic and Kinder Garden level. Well I am 62 years old today and this journey of mine started at the age of 18. And I am still doing my little baby steps. But I can say that I have found a great meaning of life and feel great sense of satisfaction and purpose in my life, and much happier with this meaning and maybe I have become a little bit more useful to the world after finding this great meaning of life in my teen age. This has been my guiding light no matter what kind of ups and downs took place in my life. I must say how fortunate it has been to have such a sun shine and greatest inspiration like His Holiness the Dalai Lama in my little and short life.

Oh La La!!! Ma Ma Miya !!!
Happy PourrrrrrR.....Ray!!!!!!!!!!!!!!!!!!!!!!!!!!!!!!!!!!!

Nawang Khechog is first Tibetan Grammy Nominee and the most renowned Tibetan flutist in the world. He has won multiple awards from Tibet, India, Nepal and United States of America. He is one of the Tibet's formost world music & spiritual music composer and also one of the first Tibetan musicians to be able to break into International music scene with his original and authentic musical compositions (solo and collaborative albums) to be distributed around the world.

Nawang was a monk for 11 years and studied Buddhist philosophy and meditation with His Holiness the Dalai Lama and many other Tibetan masters. He also lived as hermit, meditating in the Himalayan foothills for several years under the guidance of His Holiness.

Nawang received Tibetan Music Award ("Special Recognition", similar to "Life Time Achievement Award") He also received Raasrang World Flute Festival Award of India from Former president of India, Dr. A.P.G. Abdul Kalam and International Civil Golden Award, The Highest Civilian Award of Nepal and he received "The Multicultural Award" from Boulder and the Visionary Awards of Colorado, USA "Best Music of the Year" and "Best World Music".
www.NawangKhechog.com

L.I.F.E. – 'Love In Finite Expression'
by Liz Mitten Ryan

I must preface what I'm about to share with an introduction that it comes from source through a clear connection to animals and nature. I have lived on a 320 acre sacred land removed from radio, T.V. and newspapers and all their manipulation to conform with the human mass mind consciousness for 18 years.

Over that time I have discovered the field of ALL consciousness which the animals and natural world are a part of. Humans create barriers by their beliefs. Over the past 10 years I have channelled 5 books co-authored by my horses, dogs, cats and cows and produced two award-winning documentaries and dozens of YouTube videos and offer life discovering retreats to people from all over the world.

The word 'meaning' we find is a little obscure in its dictionary explanation and synonyms for it are varied. If we look at the synonyms for meaning being essence, spirit, force, content, we conclude that the meaning of life is LOVE. Without needing to interpret or understand, life just IS that force in expression in its every creative nuance.

LOVE loves and by its very nature is so vast, incomprehensible and dynamic that as all of nature we must simply surrender to its beauty, majesty and wisdom to live at one with its intuitively directed flow. We are then one with the conscious energetic field of God or the ALL upon which we are all fleeting expressions existing in a state for a moment in time, and LIFE is the continuous expression of us all. In *'Life Unbridled – What Animals Teach us About Spiritual Truth'* the animals share that L.I.F.E. is 'Love In Finite Expression', forever.

Other synonyms for 'meaning' are definition, explanation, interpretation, understanding, and they reflect the human need to intellectualize and understand. When I asked the question of why, I was given the 'The Creation Story' written through the animals perspective and on receiving it I remembered its truth. We are all the Meaning of Life.

The Creation Story:

"In the perfect realms of spirit, a group of creator Gods with blessings from the Oneness or the 'ALL' imagined and conceived a perfect planet E.A.R.T.H. (Expressing And Re-creating The Harmony) (also the same letters in H.E.A.R.T., (Holographic Expression and Re-creation Tuning device) which would contain a living, evolving library expressing the great beauty and diversity of Love In Finite Expression (L.I.F.E.), all in harmonic alignment, all interdependent, all one in the body of the ALL (The Garden of Eden story).

The Creator Gods descended from the heavens to play in their creation and returned to spirit at will. Over time the density and laws of time and space drew them deeper into their creation until some were too dense to return to spirit and chose to be part of a great experiment to see if the seeds of the Oneness planted in the good earth would ultimately grow to become the fruit and flowers of that Oneness.

The animals, minerals and plants all maintained a clear connection to the Oneness while the creator Gods or 'humans' as they became when planted in the hum-us of earth chose a veil of forgetfulness, partly to ease the deep sadness of separation from spirit and to be part of the 'blind study'. This forgetfulness encompassed the human understanding and connection to its own creation, its brothers and sisters and all the children of its own creation. The humans descended into a place of separation and aloneness broken only by a faint glimmer of a memory glimpsed in Heart felt moments of the awareness of the underlying force of unconditional Love in ALL things.

The animals and the non-human earth beings, all of us One with you in your creation, call to you to leave the cloudy confusion of your minds and join with us again in the eternal knowing of Love and Wisdom held in the Heart.

Spend unstructured time with us. Let us tune you again to the highest levels of vibration. We vibrate with the pulse of ALL creation and share the One breath of spirit that breathes through us ALL. We are All the One 'I Am' and your hope to re-connect and re-member the dream of L.I.F.E. and prove ultimately the parable that the seed planted in the good earth will multiply to become the fruit and flower of the sowers inspiration."

The Herd

Liz Mitten Ryan is a clear channel for the ALL (or God), sharing the pure outpouring of inspiration as a diverse rainbow of creativity. Through her art, books and retreats with animals and nature she seeks to allow others to re-member our connection to oneness. Wisdom, Truth, Joy, Freedom, Abundance and Love are our birthright and as we open to and share our unique gifts we can once again walk in the garden of our true purpose.

Liz and the 'Herd' have written 5 award-winning books and been the subject of 2 award winning documentaries.
www.EquinisityRetreats.com

Chao Chou's Tree
by Peter Wohl

I believe that the current interest in the question about the meaning of life reflects the deepening state of alienation that we humans are living in. I presume that our indigenous ancestors would have found this inquiry to be both irrelevant and unnecessary. Living in a seamless matrix of religion, culture, and community, all enfolded intimately with the natural world that surrounded them, people implicitly knew their place within the order of things.

Over the millennia however, we have moved further and further from that intimacy, from that place of innate knowing, that profound involvement in the complex web of existence, that is the functioning of what Zen refers to as "One Body", this profoundly interconnected universe. Now, informed by our scientific paradigm, we post-modern humans stand naked before the cold, indifferent, atomistic cosmos. Stripped in this fashion, we tiny frightened creatures are trying to find a basis for grounding and guiding our lives. Being accustomed to using our intellect as the primary tool to navigate the no longer familiar landscape of our world, we therefore ponder the meaning of our lives. The fact is though, that we cannot "think" our way out of the existential conundrum we have created for ourselves.

Still, there is a resolution. The wonderful Tang Dynasty Chan teacher Chao Chou pointed out the way to do that with great simplicity and clarity. A monk asked Chao Chou why Bodhidharma came from the west? Chao Chou replied, "The oak tree in the garden." The monk's question about the great Indian teacher's journey to China is generally taken to mean "what is the meaning of Chan Buddhism", which is essentially the same question "as what is the meaning of life". Chou Chou's response can seem enigmatic, but it's quite direct. At the first blush, he asks us to desist from all our futile intellectual endeavors, our "why" inquiries and **look, right here, right now, being aware of just This,** this Great Reality unfolding before our eyes.

But Chao Chou's tree has much more to teach us. The tree does not have any existential dilemmas; it fully expresses its being in every moment of its life. In spring the new buds burst forth, in summer it spreads its green canopy, in autumn the leaves change color and fall, and in winter its bare branches stand dormant against the darkened sky. The tree is fully engaged in life, responding appropriately to the conditions it experiences in each moment. What does that suggest to us humans? It tells us that we too must engage fully with our lives, regardless of what we may encounter. Life presents us with a panoply of conditions. Our tendency is to discriminate, to pick and choose between those we like and those we want to avoid. When we are living in that manner, we are only half alive, wasting our precious time resisting the inevitability of impermanence. When we immerse ourselves fully, the meaning of our life is inherent in the sincerity of our actions.

Furthermore, Chao Chou's amazing tree is deeply connected to all being that surrounds it. Beneath the soil it has symbiotic relationships with mycelium, nematodes, bacteria and invertebrates. Its branches are home to squirrels and birds. Its shade provides protection for the young plants emerging from the forest floor, as well as giving many beings shelter from summer's heat. When its acorns fall to the ground they feed squirrels, deer and other creatures. It removes CO_2 from the air, releasing life-giving O_2. In a sense, by simply expressing its nature as a tree, it manifests great compassion. Please understand that I am not ascribing an anthropomorphic attribute to the tree. I am suggesting that **living fully in relationship with all of Creation**, as the tree does, we are fulfilling our true nature as humans. Expressed in another way, when we are living in this way, simply and naturally expressing compassion, we are manifesting our enlightened nature.

How then do we establish this way of living in connection with the world? How do we enter and sustain profound relationships with our Mother

Earth and all of our fellow beings? The answer lies with our emotions. Our emotions are the manifestation of our connections to the world. They are the stuff that binds us to all of Creation. Without emotions we would be indifferent automatons. By opening our hearts and allowing our rich tapestry of emotions to flow freely, we are moved to acknowledge and respond to the conditions around us. That is the very essence of **living in connection**, the very essence of our true humanity.

There are some Buddhist practitioners who see the state of equanimity, that many Buddhist's aspire to, as a state of perpetual calm, resulting from the absence of emotion. I would suggest that equanimity is not the absence of emotion, but the embrace of all of our emotions, without distinguishing between those that are pleasant and those that are painful.

We Buddhists also mistrust emotions because as humans we can become addicted to the powerful emotional states, such as love, anger, and rage. However, the issue is not the emotional states themselves, but our attachment to the emotions, our addiction to those states of being. When we are neither grasping for particular emotional states, nor trying to avoid others, we are able to allow them to come and go freely. That is true equanimity, living in the world, freely allowing the ebb and flow of our many, varied emotional states.

If our hearts are open to emotional experience, we aren't able to witness the terrible suffering in the world, without feeling profound sadness, pain, grief, frustration and even anger. Those emotions can help to awaken our empathy and compassion for those who are suffering, if we can avoid making it all about **our** discomfort. Our ego wants to subjectify our experiences and we need to let go of that tendency. The discomfort of negative emotions that arise when we witness suffering will pass naturally, especially if our immediate focus is working to alleviate the suffering we are witnessing.

The pattern of our emotional experiences is much like the weather, ever-changing in response to rapidly varying conditions. Just as we cannot control whether the day will be sunny or rainy, we cannot control whether our circumstances will trigger happiness or sadness. And, just as it is a futile waste of our energy to resist the weather, it is similarly futile to despair over our emotions. We must try to see them all as clouds scudding by against the blue sky of a summer afternoon.

Perhaps the most important of our emotions is Love. In this context I am not speaking of the type of love we experience in romantic relationships, which is usually conditional, colored by our ego's needs and wants. The Love I am referring to is like the *Agape* spoken of in the New Testament, love that is unconditional and universal. It is the feeling that emerges when we have a direct encounter with the world, an encounter that is free from the usual subject-object dichotomy. It is a powerful relational experience, that exists apart from the needs and desires of our ego. That form of direct encounter is akin to Buber's experience of I-Thou. When we really experience a magnificent sunset, the song of a bird, or the humanity of another person, Love is the feeling that arises. That Love is the glue that binds us in relationship to the world.

Interestingly, while we usually think of hatred as the opposite of love, this Love exists in relationship to Grief. Grief is the emotion we experience when the being(s) or conditions we Love are lost or harmed. When we witness a forest, whose trees have been slaughtered in a clear cut, if we are awake and open, we experience Grief. When we see a homeless person on the street, if we are capable of seeing them without subjective filters, thereby experiencing our Love for them, we will also Grieve for their suffering. Just as this Love is not tied to our personal needs, our likes and dislikes, this Grief is our unconditional response to loss and suffering in the world. We are often tempted to shut down and avoid the raw discomfort of Grief, but **life in**

connection calls us to remain awake to the reality. If we are to Love the world, Grief is a natural consequence, especially in this time when our indifference and cruelty towards our fellow beings is so visibly present.

We must constantly work to allow our Love and our Grief to drive our compassion, summoning us to be agents of change in the world. The work of embracing those that are suffering, is the vital activity of **living in connection**. It is the realization of our fundamental nature as human beings.

❧❀❧

Peter Wohl is a Zen Buddhist priest and teacher at the Treetop Zen Centers in Oakland and Portland Maine. He has worked in the field of addictions treatment for over 20 years. Peter also combines his life-long love of the outdoors with principles derived from Zen practice to create workshops and trips that are designed to help people make a deep, restorative connections with the natural world. www.TreeTopZenCenter.org

A Billionaire of Love?
by Joel Solomon

Life is a blessing with rich soil to grow every possible contribution we can make with our time and resources, for a good life for people close to us, in our ecosystems, and most of all, that people 500 years from now, have far better lives.

LOVE

Life is an act of love.

Love is kindness, generosity, empathy, luminosity, and the longing for justice. It's a golden rule. It's awe of this garden of Eden, of the divine within all that exists. It's devotion to the sacred, the profound, and the enlightenment of all beings.

We continually assess our abilities, passions, and effectiveness. We commit ourselves to service, satisfaction, and support of the whole. We commit to lifelong learning, especially in our inner skills. We absorb the teachings provided by natural systems. We draw on perennial wisdoms.

How may I be a "billionaire of good deeds"? Might I become a "Billionaire of Love"?

I must work daily to know what that means, to practice, to feel, to assess, to question, to have faith, and to see. I will fall many times. I will rise yet once more again. The most poignant gives us direction.

May we find joy and peace and satisfaction. May all beings thrive. May we live on in the effervescence of luminosity that grows richer and more nourishing, with each next moment of awareness.

May we FLOW ..... and GLOW.

Because it's GAME TIME!

ALL IN.

Joel Solomon is the author of *The Clean Money Revolution: Reinventing Power, Purpose, and Capitalism*. He's the Chairman of Renewal Funds, a $98 million mission venture capital firm. He has invested in over 100 early growth-stage companies in North America, delivering above market returns while catalyzing positive social and environmental change.
www.JoelSolomon.org
www.RenewalFunds.com

The Fly, Destiny and the Meaning of Life
by Megan Hollingsworth

The question itself implies a mind that seeks and even requires meaning. And one who has lost a sense of meaning for it's own life. For each is a meaning and, thus, life's meaning in total.

The absence of meaning encourages one to question meaning. Like the absence of happiness encourages one to ask, "What is happiness?" And when one asks honestly inward, the answer not found externally, is generally clear.

So, it's helpful to begin with questioning meaning as often as necessary. Such is the uncertainty of life moment to moment and continuous. What brought meaning then is different than now because then happened. And meaning is in the happening. Meaning is momentary and of lived experience.

So, there is a beginning. Meaning may be found in losing all together a sense of one's own meaning.

My lasting honest answer is, I don't know what the meaning of life is. I see the flower. And ask, What do you make of life? What does common toad make of life? Rose? Fire ant? Big tree?

I have thought though that there is meaning in pain and pleasure. And in relationship, as I experience dynamics of an embodiment shaped by a thousand meanings determined through my actions and the actions of others.

And I have experienced a sense of fullness, like illumination, when losing sense of my own life's meaning I realized meaning through a fly's presence and an author's impulse.

One morning summer 2016 after I'd finished eating oatmeal, a fly landed on the spoon and proceeded to clean up after me. The day before, I'd read about maggots and how flies enable the scent of roses in Joanne Elizabeth Lauck's *The Voice of the Infinite In the Small: Re-imagining the Insect-Human Connection*.

Joanne's writing, which includes folk tale, provided an understanding between me and this fly. And I wept. I wept because this fly thought enough of me to share the spoon. And I, having shamed myself into isolation, a very real non-existence, had hardly ever appreciated someone's company so much.

That encounter brought a poem titled DESTINY. Since that moment, I do not shoo flies. Though I would kill a biting fly as I do biting ants. While paying attention. If I choose, I can imagine meaning in the bite. As to ask, Why do you bite me? And then listen for an answer.

So, I guess for now my thought is that meaning in life can be found in another's existence by losing meaning for one's own life through isolation.

Meaning that is *to feed someone else is to feed oneself.* And this is ultimately the case when two are not one and not two. In other words, to realize the Mother's love and be a reflection of this. A reflection that includes boundaries simply that the meaning of life may continue to be explored together.

DESTINY

And the life was dwelling
Nowhere and everywhere

And the feeling was being
Alone and crowded

And the motion was moving
Fast to be stopped
Short of a destination
Beginning again slowly
To get somewhere
Other than here

Until arriving there,
The still point of which everything arises
And for which everything gives way

Where one weeps because
someone
has thought to join
for breakfast

What is learned in school

Are but names, isolated facts and figures
That only books recall

What is retained of that learning
Is but how to dispense ketchup from a bottle

And a sense that more is missing

Until the breath is lost,
So that what it means to breathe is found.

Then realized in a mind is the privilege

That fly would see fit
To share the spoon

Elephant would trust enough
To invite his grief,

And sequoia would endow
The origin

Megan Hollingsworth, MS, is a mother, writer, and yogic practitioner with deep roots in the Religious Society of Friends (Quakers) stemming back to religious persecution in Ireland. At the close of 2011, Megan initiated Extinction Witness, a global arts project of Empowerment WORKS 501c3, to support

199

those who 'live in a world of wounds' and amplify the compassionate response to human suffering at the root of long-standing genocide and accelerated biodiversity loss and species extinction. She serves as a lead team member for Lost Species Day, November 30, which offers a chance each year to learn about extinct and critically endangered species, lifeways, and ecological communities, and engage in practical helpful action. With guidance from colleagues, Megan has authored a Vow 2 Act recently published in Unpsychology Magazine's Climate Minds Anthology.

www.WailDance.com
www.MeganHollingsworth.com

The Meaning of Life... that Extends Beyond Language
by Sharmila Desai

In honest humility I find the meaning of life to be a mystery. I embrace the unknown for it nurtures us all to search and to strive in the world, embarking on a lifetime devoted to the pursuit of truth.

Life's mysticism reveals itself as we seek it's meaning. We are the artist in our own self portrait while at the same time we are humbled by a higher force pre-embedded within the design. In our search, continuous and omniscient, we have experiences that return us to the pulse of the present moment to the breathing quality that is all of life. In this unifying realization that we are the same and one, infinite and limitless, a tender sweetness shines forth. We connect with our heart feeling the presence of God everywhere.

The quest to find the answer starts at a source within. As we dive deeper into ourselves we begin to experience an interconnectedness to all around us – other people, animals, nature, the cosmos. A magical unfolding automatically happens from tapping into the divine energy that lives in us to that which exists everywhere and is eternal. From experiencing life's interwoven nature we show our appreciation for the gift of life through service, compassion and gratitude.

The vastness of life's essence and the glimpses we are able to grasp extends beyond language. It is in the simplicity of coming home to our body and breath, tuning into the original silence within, that we can begin to evoke an understanding on what the meaning of life is.

৵৶৸৶

Sharmila Desai is a mother, author, yoga practitioner and KPJAYI Certified Ashtanga yoga teacher. She comes from a matrilineal line of renowned Indian classical dancers and intellectuals who raised her with the importance of spiritual discipline and ancient art in contemporary daily life. On graduating from Columbia University, Sharmila was awarded the Henry Evans Fellowship to set up a dance program for street children in Mumbai, India. Believing in the importance of Seva as part of spiritual practice, she has also taught yoga therapy workshops internationally and runs a community garden at her children's school.

The Eternal Light
by Solomon Katz

As a ray of light shined through a prism diffracts into a spectrum of color, the Eternal Light, when shined through the body, diffracts into the spectrum of the five senses and world perception.

The purpose of life is to abide as the Eternal Light which, when shined through the body, projects the world. However, when the Eternal Light identifies with the body through which it shines it becomes an ego, mis-taking itself to be that distinct body/mind through which it shines, separate from the world which it perceives as outside and other, as if the perceived world and its actors were not themselves projections of the Eternal Light.

The ego, the separate entity which goes by the name you are called, then becomes involved in its stories, the drama of life, the drama of desire directed toward objects of the world.

To abide as the Eternal Light – this is the process of spiritual awakening – attention must be withdrawn from preoccupation with the temporal story lines of desire that comprise the mind and ego. Attention comes to rest in its source and fundamental nature as the Eternal Light. Then it can truly be said that, *"God is never distant, absent, or other."* God is all there is; All God All the Time; it is Never Not God.

The mind is the locus of preoccupation with the world and thus the locus of suffering. What remains when the mind, ego, and suffering are abandoned into the purity of stillness? Joy and delight in the beauty of the Eternal Light and its manifestations.

But this joy arises, again, with stillness of mind. Stillness requires a renunciation of everything that is not the Eternal Light, and so amounts to supreme devotion to Truth, at the expense of worldliness and illusion. When the mind is purified of all content only the Eternal Light remains.

How do we know that this is the purpose of life? Because, while preoccupied with the world and desire directed toward the world, there is a feeling of unease. Something feels out of sorts. I am seeking something that the world of impermanence never can provide. The feeling of unease abates when the natural condition – what in the East is called *sahaja* – is restored. In the natural condition the feeling of unease, of being out of sorts is finally relieved. I have returned home. Like a carpenter's level, the bubble is finally aligned perfectly to center, to the Heart. Anything other than home – the Heart, the natural condition, sahaja – will feel off; incomplete and unsatisfactory.

The meaning of life, then, is not something that I know as an object, it is experiential. I *am* the meaning of life. And the paradox is that this meaning is both entirely at hand, as close and self evident as existence itself, and entirely transcendent in being pristine, beyond all content.

I am, and I am beyond all particulars. Not this particular body/mind that arises at this particular time in this particular world appearance. Not the details of this particular movie, but something transcendent and absolute: I am emptiness and fullness, nothing and everything, boundless, timeless, and yet as close as close can be, as close as this moment, as intimate as this moment and yet vast, for when the mind is empty of stories, nothing remains to obstruct the natural state of the Heart which is completely full... with love.

For Love is the nature of the brimming Heart. Anything other than love, the brimming Heart, feels lacking and we will be compelled to correct, to realign to love, where the journey joyfully recognizes its culmination.

❧⁂❧

A child of Holocaust survivors, **Solomon Katz** was fluent in the Jewish tradition and biblical Hebrew at an early age. His interest in meditation led him to Asia where he lived as a Buddhist monk in Myanmar and Sri Lanka. By the time he returned home and began doctoral studies, he had spent three years in periods of silent meditation retreat. At Harvard University he earned concurrent graduate degrees in world religion and psychology. He trained and held a clinical faculty position in psychology at Harvard Medical School. He is the author of *"Beauty as a State of Being,"* winner of several book awards, and the forthcoming *"Where Time and Story End: Verses on Eternal Truth."*

He lives in Harvard, Massachusetts where he and his wife raised a family of four beautiful girls, many animals, and many fruit trees planted over the years at which he loves to gaze, often with the teachings of Ramana Maharshi in hand.
www.SolomonKatz.com

Loving Kindness – The True Core of Life
by Dr. Hansaji Jayadeva Yogendra

"Reflect and Ponder on the true nature of life; it is love!"

During my regular session at The Yoga Institute, one of the students was asked according to him what is the meaning of life? He answered life is B and D. Means life is "B" =birth to "D" =death. But I interjected there is more to life than "B" & "D" in between there is "C". Let me explain — "C" is choice, and we have the power of choice.

You have a choice. Life is beautiful — make your actions and experiences accordingly. Problems come in our life to teach us. Choose to be a learner from those experiences. Become stronger more capable rather than becoming weak.

Everything depends on how you live your life. We can make or break our own lives. Gifted with nimble minds, we can either choose to suffer in life because of others or choose to be happy no matter what!

Today superficial goals of losing weight, no wrinkles, getting rich quickly are defining the meaning of life. We are in a technologically advanced age and want quick fix solutions for everything. All these goals take us further away from our true inner self. We end up looking outside for happiness. This kind of happiness is for a very short while. Every life's existence and journey is different. While it is okay to learn few life lessons from other's life experience remember to exercise caution. Life is not at all one-size-solution-that-fits everyone.

There is divinity within everyone of us.

Dynamically, we are all connected to every consciousness, human being, plants, animals and even the tiniest molecule which is omnipresent. The whole universe is vibrating and connected with energy. Therefore, have a positive relationship and an impact on everything and everyone around. Naturally, this gives our lives true meaning. Grab every opportunity and align yourselves harmoniously through positive thoughts, words, deeds and actions. Choose kindness and love to create harmony and enhance your own life's meaning.

When you see things carefully you realize the really beautiful, peaceful and successful people's lives rotate around love. Yoga by itself means union; when a union of two people happen due to love, life starts.

Love is visible in caring concern, friendly attitude, sincerity, and duty; all these concepts reflect love. In animal kingdom strong overpower the weak. But in humans strong protect the weak, cares for the weak, thus duty is nothing else but love.

Love is a *Bhava*. It is a powerful emotion which has the glimpse of the higher consciousness. Yoga has a belief of '*bhavas*', which means feelings. Yoga Sutra advocates *Maitri Bhava*, which means a feeling of friendliness or benevolence. It is "unattached loving kindness."

Externally, a person may not appear loving, but his intention, his *bhava*, is more important. External behavior is misleading. Someone who wishes you ill may be an excellent actor and appear very friendly and loving towards you.

In Vedas, a statement states, 'Lord, let me not face a person who is externally different and internally different.' It is difficult to manage with such a double-faced person. There are examples of a couple fooling innocent people in a train with their friendliness and then disappearing with their belongings when they go to have a drink of water at the platform, or feeding them medicated food that puts them to sleep and disappearing with their belongings. Today, all this cleverness is happening in the world. We are taken in by such show of love and friendliness, but instead, we should be indifferent to external show and go more by the internal intention of a person.

Each one of us is born with inherent two traits: *care* and *love*. Have you seen a child play with a doll or puppy? Here you see love and care in the purest form. So we could learn from children and keep caring the fundamental core of love.

We should not develop feelings of hatred towards others. Our internal reality ends up being expressed in the external world through vibrations and in turn, we attract antagonistic vibrations to ourselves. Similarly, we should not be affected by someone else's negativity. We should maintain our loving friendliness. We could learn this kind of loving kindness from children.

It is your life, and only you can decide — the true meaning of your life. Once you decide, don't look back even if it is not the set norm!

❧

Yoga Guru Dr. Smt. Hansaji Jayadeva Yogendra, director of The Yoga Institute — an exemplary yogi and a scholar transforming millions of lives worldwide. She learnt and taught yoga at a time when women were not considered a part of the Yoga fraternity. Smt. Hansaji played a pivotal role in making key changes in India Central Government's policies to further the cause of Yoga awareness and spread the message of holistic health and peace through Yoga for the wellbeing of humanity. She's the author of more than ten books and recipient of endless awards.
www.TheYogaInstitute.org

Wait For Her
by Mahmoud Darwish

Wait for her with an azure cup.
Wait for her in the evening at the spring, among
perfumed roses.
Wait for her with the patience of a horse trained for
mountains.
Wait for her with the distinctive, aesthetic taste of a
prince.
Wait for her with seven pillows of cloud.
Wait for her with strands of womanly incense
wafting.
Wait for her with the manly scent of sandalwood
on horseback.
Wait for her and do not rush.

If she arrives late, wait for her.
If she arrives early, wait for her.
Do not frighten the birds in her braided hair.
Wait for her to sit in a garden at the peak of its
flowering.
Wait for her so that she may breathe this air, so
strange to her heart.
Wait for her to lift her garment from her leg, cloud
by cloud.
And wait for her.

Take her to the balcony to watch the moon
drowning in milk.

Wait for her and offer her water before wine.
Do not glance at the twin partridges sleeping on
her chest.
Wait and gently touch her hand as she sets a cup on
marble.
As if you are carrying the dew for her, wait.
Speak to her as a flute would to a frightened violin
string,
as if you knew what tomorrow would bring.

Wait, and polish the night for her ring by ring.
Wait for her until Night speaks to you thus:
There is no one alive but the two of you.
So take her gently to the death you so desire,
and wait.

❧❧❧

Mahmoud Darwish was a Palestinian poet and
author who was regarded as the Palestinian
national poet. He won numerous awards for his
works.

The Path of Love
by OM C. Parkin

What is the meaning of life?

"To know who you really are." Know your SELF. Once and for ever.

Many years ago my master gave me this answer. It is the final answer to this question. Who receives this answer by a master of the path and can hear it with the heart, has come to the end of the search.

Many answers had preceded this final one, some intelligent and eloquent, many compassionate, warm-hearted and human. But none came close to this final one. It is simple, unconditional, radical. It is Death. The invitation to die for a separate entity called "I".

BEING, Consciousness, Bliss (satchitananda). This *Trinity* in Oneness is the natural state of the human being. The state of the human being knowing him/herSELF.

The great spiritual paths of humanity, the Path of Truth and the Path of Love, both end in satchitananda. The meaningless meaning of life.

Can you say something about love?*

How can I speak of love? I can only tell you what love is not. I would say that next to the concept of enlightenment, love is the most misunderstood concept, for love, as well as enlightenment, cannot be grasped by any concept.

What can I tell you about love that you won't make into a concept? Love is neither an emotion nor a feeling.

The other day an Osho disciple took my words in Darshan and said, "All you say sounds so intellectual, but I miss love!" I replied that love *is,* in this moment, and it is the love out of which Darshan occurs. Like many seekers, he had a sentimental concept of love, and this concept stood between him and the teacher, between him and *himSelf.* When the mind speaks of love, it is mostly speaking about sentimentality.

What you search for is that which does not pass. States pass and feelings pass. If love were a feeling, it would pass. Love can only be found in *That* which does not pass, and *That* which does not pass is nothing that can be perceived. It is *That* which perceives. And *That* which perceives is *That* which you *are.* And *That* which you are has no definable facets by which love can be confined.

Love has no polarity. It is nothing that can be described. Everything that comes out of the Self *is* love. A fit of anger can equally come out of the Self and that fit of anger equally occurs in love. In the moment that any concept, any past, or any future fall away, in that moment, love *is*.

How will you measure love? The moment you say, "Love looks like this but not like that," you've lost it.

There are many spiritual teachings about love. They teach how it is to be in love and how it is not to be in love; what love means, what love doesn't mean, and what love forbids. Those are only concepts about love, not *love itself*. There is no need for a teaching about love. All that is needed is the recognition of your true Self, and in this recognition, love is realized. Which form love will take, who knows?

*What is love, really?**

In Advaita, the teaching of non-duality, little is said about love. The reason is that anything connected with the notion of love has nothing to do with love or has to do as much or as little with love as everything else. What the mind takes for love is hormone release. No concept of love could be understood by the mind. As long as there is the slightest idea of what Love is, there is also an idea of what Love is not, or, more truthfully, what Love is not allowed to be. *Love* is that there is peace, and Love is that wars are waged.

I could tell you a lot about what love is not. It does not mean being just a certain way. Love cannot be touched by any idea. There is no one more or less loving than anyone else. Love has nothing to do with anything belonging to the personality. There is nothing individual about love. It has nothing to do with relationship. Everything that arises, arises out of love.

*Excerpts from OM C. Parkin *'The Birth of the Lion'*.

⁂

OM C. Parkin, mystic, philosopher and author. Director of the Contemporary Inner School in Germany.

OM embodies in his work the link between Eastern non-duality and Christian mysticism, of depth psychology and philosophy, beyond the limits of religions and confessions. In the course of this, he often refers to the tradition of advaita, which has been revived in the 20th century by Shri Ramana Maharshi, Shri H.W.L. Poonja, the American Gangaji and others (neo advaita). OM acts in the tradition of these teachers and by rooted in early Christian teaching. His work in the tradition of silence can be described by three functions: teacher (of wisdom), healer (of the soul), seer (of the heart). www.kloster-saunstorf.de/en

The Breath, the Heartbeat, and the Meaning of Life
by Rosalyn W. Berne

In my early childhood I encountered the spirits of people who were deceased. This taught me that there is something really special about being alive; that human life on Earth is precious, as it gives our souls an opportunity to have learning experiences, such that we might eventually remember who we truly are. Such experiences also deepened my sense of mystery about life, such that I'm not entirely sure I know what *life* is, let alone its meaning. In that context, I offer a few reflections on the clearest meanings I have come to understand:

First, that the breath of life is something we share with every other breathing being, which is one means by which all of life is connected. I recall the time my husband and I visited Papallacta; a small town in Ecuador located at 10,600 feet in the Andes. I had the horrifying sensation of not getting enough oxygen from the air, until I noticed some birds moving in a grove of trees. I was calmed in realizing that while trees do use oxygen, they release more than they take in. And those birds were breathing. I got the sense that the trees, the birds, and I were all breathing, together. My understanding of breathing expanded even further when I visited Arenal volcano in Costa Rica and heard the rhythmic sound of gases expelled from its active cone. I was stirred to tears, feeling that volcano was "breathing," with me, and that Earth itself is alive.

Second, that human life is a beating heart. Right after her birth, I held my daughter Zoe in my arms as she struggled for breath, her heart beating, but faintly. She lived only three days after that, and with her dying I began to glean that being alive gives us the capacity to learn what it is to love. Through the suffering, which is inevitable with living, the meaning of my own life has been to learn what it is to love, but also that this awareness is fleeting.

Deeper than the breath and the heartbeat that sustain our lives, is the indwelling spirit. On any given day, especially if the air is fresh, the sky is clear, the breeze is balmy, and my loved ones are doing well, I sense the pure joy of being alive in this body-self. But when my attention is on the pain and anguish that life can bring, I may feel at a loss for why I, or any of us, is here on this earth. In those times, if I can shift into inner silence, sensing into and beyond my flowing breath and beating heart, I can find the stillness that reminds me that what I AM, is love. My daily challenge (and perhaps the meaning of my own life) is to remember that!

Rosalyn W. Berne, Ph.D. is an associate professor at the University of Virginia, where she explores the intersecting realms between emerging technologies, science, fiction and myth, and between the human and non-human worlds. Her writing and teaching focus on engineering and society, and ethics in technological development. Beyond her academic life, she has authored books in the body/mind/spirit genre, which explore spiritual growth arising from encounters with animals and other beings.
www.RosalynBerne.com

Dare to Be Fully Alive... Make Love Your Quest
by Ana Forrest & Jose Calarco

It is our task as spiritual beings to remove the blocks that inhibit the native joy and passions of our spirit; we must delve deeply into our own mysterious being and begin to rediscover our poetic voice & soul.

To become courageous spirits, we must loosen our character from its rigid boundaries and habitual patterns, and begin to express ourselves with joyful abandon, and without fear.

The fear of life can sometimes be intoxicating; there are dangers, obstacles and grief in every direction, and we tend to become prisoners of mediocrity, monotony and detachment who have damaged the radiant connection to life.

Our response is to crawl away and disappear; we think if we are not seen, then perhaps we will be safe?

Disobey your fear and dare to be fully alive in such a world; tap into the spontaneous forces of the present moment unclouded by your gloomy history, and begin leaving your charm and imprint wherever you go.

Remember there is no greater pain than unfulfilled potential.

Begin to see the world through the eyes of the heart. Give up trying to find yourself and dare being yourself. Cultivate a great sense of humor on your journey, and remember laughter is the language of the Gods. Your life is as magical or as dull as you make it.

Love is the spirit of the moonlight, the desire of the sunlight: it holds all the mysteries of the night and intention of the Stars. Love directs the four winds, is the eye of the storm and the fragrance of the flower. Love is the song of the shoreless sea and playfulness of the rolling waves; it's the mistress of the sky and devotee of the Earth. Love is the rain falling from Heaven scattering its pearls from the silky clouds. Love inspires Mountains to reach great heights; it is the essence of the forest and the impulse of nature.

Love is the touchstone of creativity, the devotion within music, and the fire of discovery; Love is the hidden treasure lying underneath our ruins and is the remedy for all afflictions.

Now that love has pierced my very depths, I have no companion but Love; I am beckoned to its every call.

Make Love your quest; it is the only worthy pilgrimage for the Heart.

When I participate in Love, I merge with my beloved and our Spirit's go wandering upon the wind embraced by God's majesty.

PS...Take responsibility for your own evolution and don't die with the music left inside.

❦❦❦

Ana Forrest is an inspiration. She has been changing people's lives for over 40 years and is an internationally-recognized pioneer in yoga and emotional healing. Ana is a Medicine Woman, the creatrix of Forrest Yoga and author of the highly-acclaimed book, *Fierce Medicine.*

Jose Calarco has had a long and varied association in the Arts, Music and Yoga in Australia and around the World for the last thirty years. In this time he has covered almost the entire spectrum of experience, from producer and administrator of large-scale events, to innovative artistic direction in the fields of Dance, Film, Theatre, Yoga and Music.

In 2014 Jose joined forces with international yoga legend Ana Forrest as a ceremonial musical director, business mentor, and Ana's life partner, providing artistic and cultural direction into Ana's international yoga events. Jose is a singer, songwriter, musician, storyteller and Medicine man. Jose and Ana's Synergetic Collision of worlds is today reshaping the future of Yoga.
www.ForrestYoga.com

Going HOME Empty
by Kurtis Lamkin

The meaning of life?

To go Home empty. To rassle receiving to the ground so we can fill our waking days with giving. We come into the world buck-naked, but we are full. The heaven is to go back battered bone-dry and completely empty of everything we were put into the world to give.

It's intimidating to look out across the land and water and among the stars, and then challenge ourselves to fill the entire space with the little bit of truth we have in our new bodies. It's alright. The center of us is infinite. As tiny as we are we matter just as much as any phenomenon that roars or burns in the universe.

The ancestors who fill us and wait for us to come home first dressed us and advise us to carry ourselves well in the world. For some the world ends at their village's edge; others may be swept away across oceans. Either way we carry ourselves and when we keep ourselves to ourselves we waste and rot.

So give, as if it is the last chance to be alive.... What else can we bring back to those who put the love into us but complete, naked, hungry emptiness?

Kurtis Lamkin is a contemporary American embodiment of the ancient West African griot tradition, which blurs the boundaries between poet, singer and storyteller. Kurt has performed internationally on stage, radio, film, and television, and was one of the featured poets in the Bill Moyers documentary, *Fooling With Words*. He also hosted MultiKultiMove, a reading series featuring writers from around the world, and produced a radio series called, "Living Proof: Contemporary Black Literature."

Becoming Love
by Dena Merriam

We each enter life with desires, goals, and challenges to overcome, and we choose birth conditions that will best help us meet these objectives. Arriving with dreams from the past that are seeking fulfillment, we find meaning as we are able to satisfy these karmic imperatives from the past, through relationship, work, artistic endeavor, etc. But these transient experiences will not satisfy us because even the most beautiful human experience ultimately disappoints. As quickly as it arrives, it disappears into the karmic mist.

We are more than our human bodies and to find the true meaning of life is to know ourselves as eternal beings, formed out of love, formed for love, and formed to spread love. That is our nature and source of lasting joy.

As we fulfill many of the objectives we have set for ourselves — finding the perfect mate, the perfect job, the perfect home, the perfect friend, having the perfect children, etc., and we still don't find complete satisfaction, we begin to look deeper for meaning that is not attached to any cause, for a joy that comes from being, not having or doing. We yearn for a state of joy, peace and complete contentment, and a love that just is, a pure state of unconditioned love where you know yourself to be one with, not separate from, all that is. To enter this state of being is the true meaning and purpose of life. Then we know who and why we are.

When we align with our true nature, the essence of who we are — beyond personality, qualities, skills, likes and dislikes – then every act, every thought, every interaction provides meaning. This is a work of many, many lifetimes. The more we learn to dance with life, to be in it but also above it, to disregard the distractions that tug at us, to live in a state of love, the closer we will come to our true purpose.

Although we may not achieve that state in this life, the search for it and the striving will bring us ever closer.

❧❧❧

Dena Merriam is the author of *My Journey Through Time: A Spiritual Memoir of Life, Death and Rebirth.* Ms. Merriam began working in the interfaith movement in the late 1990s when she served as Vice Chair of the Millennium World Peace Summit of Religious and Spiritual Leaders held at the United Nation. She subsequently convened a meeting of women religious and spiritual leaders at the Palais des Nations in Geneva and from that gathering founded the Global Peace Initiative of Women in 2002, an organization chaired by a multi-faith group of women spiritual leaders. www.gpiw.org

The Grand Reunion
by Natalie Ai Kamauu

I refuse to suppose that I am here on this Earth by happen chance. When I look at the miracle of my hands, when my ears capture the sound of rushing wind in its hollow, when I taste the salt of sea spray on my lips and smell my baby's sweet, clean breath, I am certain I am here for a divine purpose.

We are destined to be completely, undeniably different and yet, we are exactly the same. We are born. We die. What we do with the time we are given, no matter how long or short, in between these two remarkable events defines our success in this, our mortal probation.

We were formed to have distinct strengths and weaknesses so that we would depend on one another, to intertwine our talents, multiplying our abilities, repressing our frailties. We were crafted to need each other.

If my life on Earth is merely about me alone, I would be here alone. I am not. I am meant to be here with you and you and you, to be your student and your teacher, to care and to be cared for by you. I am here to first be held, to crawl, then walk and run. I am here to carry you. I am here to absorb and to grow and to stretch beyond what I think is capable. I am here to learn from you. I am here to fall and get up, fall and get up again. I am here to stand by you. I am here to feel joy and happiness, sadness and pain. To taste the bitter and the sweet. I am here to know the difference. I am here to love and to fall in love and be loved and within that bond of love to create love. I am here because of love. And so are you.

If our bodies turn to dust when our last breath we take, why should any of this matter? Why do I matter? Why do you? The faith that there will be a grand reunion of matter and light burns within me, giving me hope that this life is but a steppingstone to something far greater, something though to earn, to achieve. The belief that there is more for me after this life urges me to strive to do and be better daily. I am indeed a part of a magnificent plan designed with me in mind, designed with you in mind, every minute particle precisely in its own place. I am in my place. Of this I am sure.

***

Natalie Ai Kamauu — *"the most beautiful voice to come out of Hawai'i...."*
Grammy Nominated, Three time Female Vocalist and Miss Aloha Hula.
www.NatalieAiKamauu.com

Rumi: What Shall I Be?

I have again and again grown like grass
I have experienced seven hundred and seventy molds

I died from mineralogy and became vegetable
and from vegetativeness I died and became animal
I died from animality and became man
Then why fear disappearance thru death?

Next time I shall die
Bringing forth wings and feathers like angels

After that soaring higher than angels
What you cannot imagine
I shall be that.

The end of love is endless...

CPSIA information can be obtained
at www.ICGtesting.com
Printed in the USA
LVHW08s1832300718
585375LV00001B/93/P